Nick Vandome

Laptops
for Seniors

8th edition
for all laptops with Windows 11

In easy steps is an imprint of In Easy Steps Limited
16 Hamilton Terrace · Holly Walk · Leamington Spa
Warwickshire · United Kingdom · CV32 4LY
www.ineasysteps.com

Eighth Edition

Notice of Liability
Every effort has been made to ensure that this book contains accurate
and current information. However, In Easy Steps Limited and the
author shall not be liable for any loss or damage suffered by readers
as a result of any information contained herein.

Trademarks
Microsoft® and Windows® are registered trademarks of Microsoft
Corporation. All other trademarks are acknowledged as belonging to
their respective companies.

In Easy Steps Limited supports The Forest Stewardship Council (FSC),
the leading international forest certification organization. All our titles
that are printed on Greenpeace approved FSC certified paper carry the
FSC logo.

MIX
Paper from
responsible sources
FSC® C020837

Printed and bound in the United Kingdom

ISBN 978-1-84078-943-0

Contents

1 Choosing a Laptop 7

A Brief History of Laptops	8
Laptops v. Desktops	10
Types of Laptops	11
Laptop Jargon Explained	12
Size and Weight	14
Getting Comfortable	15
Carrying a Laptop	18
Keyboard and Touchpad	19
Using an External Mouse	20
Ports and Slots	21
The Wonder of Wireless	22
Cleaning a Laptop	23
Choosing a Carry Case	24
Spares and Accessories	25

2 Around a Laptop 27

Opening Up and Turning On	28
Touchscreen Laptops	29
About Windows	30
Obtaining Windows 11	31
New Features in Windows 11	32
The Start Button	34
The Start Menu	36
Pinning Items	39
The Desktop and Taskbar	40
Shutting Down	41
Using a Microsoft Account	42
Personalization	44
Lock Screen Settings	48
Using Themes	50
Changing Color Themes	52
Screen Resolution	54
Adjusting Volume	55
USB Flashdrives	56

3   Getting Up and Running   57

Sign-in Options   58
Settings   60
Searching   62
Setting Up Cortana   64
Using Cortana   65
Viewing Notifications   68
Opening File Explorer   70
Quick Access in File Explorer   71
File Explorer Menu Bar   73

4   Working with Apps   75

Starting with Apps   76
Windows 11 Apps   78
Using Windows 11 Apps   80
Closing Apps   82
Searching for Apps   83
Using the Microsoft Store   84
Buying Apps   87
Viewing Your Apps   88
Installing and Uninstalling Apps   89

5   The Online World   91

Introducing the Edge Browser   92
Smart Address Bar   93
Setting a Homepage   94
Using Tabs   95
Managing Tabs   96
Bookmarking Web Pages   98
Viewing Favorites   99
Collections in Edge   100
Shopping Online   102
Booking a Vacation   104
Setting Up Mail   106

Working with Mail 108
Using OneDrive 110
OneDrive Settings 113
Finding People 114
Using the Calendar 116

6 **A Digital Lifestyle** **119**

Viewing Photos 120
Editing Photos 122
Groove Music 124
Playing Music 125
Viewing Movies and TV 126
Gaming with Windows 11 128

7 **On Vacation** **129**

Transporting Your Laptop 130
Keeping Your Laptop Safe 131
Temperature Extremes 132
Laptops at Sea 133
Power Sockets 134
Airport Security 135
Keeping in Touch with Chat 136

8 **Sharing with Your Family** **139**

About Multiple Users 140
Adding Users 142
Family Safety 144

9   Networking and Wireless   149

Network Components	150
Going Wireless	151
Connecting to a Network	152
Viewing Network Status	154
Sharing Settings	155
Nearby Sharing	156
Network Troubleshooting	158

10   Battery Issues   159

Types of Battery	160
Power Consumption	161
Battery Management	162
Battery Saver	164
Charging the Battery	165
Removing the Battery	166
Dead and Spare Batteries	167
Battery Troubleshooting	168

11   System and Security   169

Privacy	170
Troubleshooting	172
System Properties	174
Cleaning Up Your Disk	176
Windows Update	178
Backing Up	181
System Restore	182
Windows Security	184

Index   187

1 Choosing a Laptop

More and more computer users are now using laptops because of their convenience and portability. This chapter looks at some of the issues to consider when buying a laptop, and how to ensure you buy the right one for your needs. It also covers the elements of a laptop and some of the accessories you will need.

8   A Brief History of Laptops

10   Laptops v. Desktops

11   Types of Laptops

12   Laptop Jargon Explained

14   Size and Weight

15   Getting Comfortable

18   Carrying a Laptop

19   Keyboard and Touchpad

20   Using an External Mouse

21   Ports and Slots

22   The Wonder of Wireless

23   Cleaning a Laptop

24   Choosing a Carry Case

25   Spares and Accessories

Apple has an excellent range of laptops, running its macOS operating system. However, the majority of this book deals with "IBM-compatible" laptops, as they are known. These types of laptops are the most common, and run on the Windows operating system.

The New icon pictured above indicates a new or enhanced feature introduced on laptops with Windows 11.

A Brief History of Laptops

Modern computers have come a long way since the days of mainframe computers, which took up entire rooms and were generally only the domain of large educational establishments or government organizations. Before microprocessors (the chips that are used to run modern-day computers), these mainframe computers were usually operated by punchcards: the operators programmed instructions via holes in a punchcard and then waited for the results, which could take hours or days.

The first personal computers – i.e. ones in which all of the computing power was housed in a single box – started to appear in the early 1970s, and the first machine that bore any resemblance to modern personal computers was called the Datapoint 2200. The real breakthrough for personal computers came with the introduction of microprocessors – small chips that contained all of the necessary processing power for the computer. After this, the industry expanded at a phenomenal rate with the emergence of major worldwide companies such as Microsoft, Apple, IBM, Dell and Intel.

But even as personal computers were being developed for a mass-market audience, there was a concerted drive to try to create a portable computer so that people could take their own computer with them wherever they went. Even in the fast-moving world of technology, the timescale for shrinking a computer from the size of a large room to the size of a small briefcase was a dramatic one.

First portable computers

With most types of technology, we are obsessed with the idea of making the item as small as possible, whether it is a music player, a telephone or a computer. However, the first portable computers bore little resemblance to the machines that we now know as laptops. At the beginning of the 1980s there were a few portable computers released, but most of them were bulky, had very small screens and could not run on internal batteries. The most popular of these was called the Osborne 1, which was released in 1981. Although this was the size of a small suitcase and had a minuscule amount of computing power compared with modern machines, it proved a big success as it enabled people to carry their computers around with them for the first time.

The machine that first used the term "laptop" was called the Gavilan SC, which was developed in 1983 and introduced in 1984. This had the big advantage of being able to run on an internal battery, and it was also one of the first portable computers that appeared with the now-universal "clamshell" design, where the monitor folded down over the keyboard.

In the late 1980s, companies such as Kyocera, Tandy, Olivetti, NEC, IBM, Toshiba, Compaq and Zenith Data Systems began developing faster and more powerful laptops, and it is in this period that the growth of laptops really began to take off.

In 1991, Apple introduced its PowerBook range of laptops, and in 1995 the introduction of Windows 95 provided a widely used operating system for IBM-compatible laptops.

Laptops have now become an integral part of the computer market, and in many areas sales have outstripped those of desktop computers. Also, they are more than capable of comfortably meeting the computing needs of most computer users. Add to this their portability (which has reached a stage where you no longer need to worry about causing yourself an injury in order to carry one around), and it is clear why laptops have become so popular.

Mobility is now an essential part of computing, and when Windows 8 was released it was aimed firmly at the mobile world. However, this caused some issues, particularly with users of desktop and laptop computers. Since then, these issues have been addressed by subsequent versions of Windows, and Windows 11 has a number of features that are aimed more at users with a traditional keyboard and mouse. This shows that laptops still have an important role to play, and will continue to do so.

Because of their size and weight, the first portable computers, such as the Osborne 1, were known rather unflatteringly as "luggables".

Laptops v. Desktops

When considering buying a laptop computer, one of the first considerations is how it will perform in comparison with a desktop computer. In general, you will pay more for a laptop with similar specifications to a desktop. The reason for this is purely down to size: it is more expensive to fit the required hardware into a laptop than the more generous physical capacity of a desktop computer. However, with modern computing technology and power, even laptops with lower specifications than their desktop cousins will be able to handle all but the most intensive computing needs of most home users. The one situation where laptops will need to have as high a specification as possible is if you are going to be doing a lot of video downloading and editing, such as converting and editing old family movies.

Some issues to consider when looking at the differences between laptops and desktops are:

- **Portability**. Laptops easily win over desktops in this respect, but when looking at this area it is worth thinking about how portable you actually want your computer to be. If you want to mainly use it in the home, then you may think that a desktop is the answer. However, a laptop gives you portability in the home too, which means that you can use your computer in a variety of locations within the home and even in the garden, if desired.

- **Power**. Even the most inexpensive laptops have enough computing power to perform most of the tasks that the majority of users require. However, if you want to have the same computing power as the most powerful desktops, then you will have to pay a comparatively higher price.

- **Functionality**. Again, because of their size, desktops have more room for items such as DVD writers, multi-card readers and webcams. These can be included with laptops, but this can also increase the price and the weight of the laptop.

Don't forget

Another issue with laptops is battery power, which is required to keep them operating when they are removed from a mains electrical source. Obviously, this is not an issue that affects desktops.

Types of Laptops

To meet the needs of the different types of people who use laptops, there are several variations that are available:

- **Netbooks**. These are the ultimate in small laptops, but have less power and functionality than larger options. They generally have screens that are approximately 10 inches (measured diagonally from corner to corner) and are best suited for surfing the web and sending email, although they can also do productivity tasks.

- **Ultrabooks**. These are very light and slim laptops that still have significant power and functionality. They have screens of approximately 13 inches, and weigh as little as 1.2 kg. They are an excellent option if you are going to be using your laptop a lot while traveling.

- **Notebooks**. These are the most common types of laptops as they have a good combination of size, weight and power. They generally have screens that are approximately 13-17 inches and weigh approximately 2-3.5 kg. Notebooks are an excellent option for using in the home and also while traveling.

- **Desktop replacements**. These are larger, heavier laptops that can be used in the home instead of a desktop computer. They are more powerful than other types of laptops, but they are not as portable. They generally have screens that are up to approximately 17-19 inches, and weigh approximately 4-6 kg.

- **Hybrids**. With the proliferation of touchscreen mobile computing devices such as smartphones and tablet computers, manufacturers have been looking at ways to incorporate this functionality into laptops. This has resulted in the development of touchscreen laptops and hybrid devices, which can be used both as a laptop and a tablet. This is done by including a keyboard that can be hidden (by having a sliding, detachable or revolving screen) so that the device can quickly be converted into a touchscreen tablet. These devices are becoming increasingly popular.

Beware

Netbooks usually have a slimmed-down version of the full Windows operating system, due to limits of their memory and architecture.

Laptop Jargon Explained

Since laptops are essentially portable computers, much of the jargon is the same as for a desktop computer. However, it is worth looking at some of this jargon and the significance it has in terms of laptops:

- **Processor**. Also known as the central processing unit, or CPU, this refers to the processing of digital data as it is provided by programs on the computer. The more powerful the processor, the quicker the data is interpreted.

- **Memory**. This closely relates to the processor and is also known as random-access memory, or RAM. Essentially, this type of memory manages the programs that are being run and the commands that are being executed. The more memory there is, the quicker programs will run. With more RAM, they will also be more stable and less likely to crash. In the current range of laptops, memory is measured in megabytes (MB) or gigabytes (GB).

- **Storage**. This refers to the amount of digital information that the laptop can store. In the current range of laptops, storage is measured in GB. There are no external signs of processor or memory on a laptop but details are available from within the **This PC** option, which is accessed from File Explorer (see page 70).

Don't forget

Memory can be thought of as a temporary storage device, as it only keeps information about currently open programs. Storage is more permanent, as it keeps the information even when the laptop has been turned off.

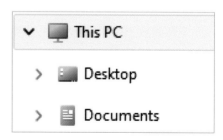

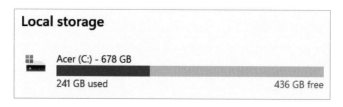

- **Optical drive**. This is a drive on the laptop that is capable of reading information from, and copying it to, a disc such as a CD or a DVD. Some modern laptops have internal optical drives such as CD writers or DVD writers, although this is becoming less common.

- **Connectivity**. This refers to the different types of media device to which the laptop can be connected. These include card readers for memory cards from digital cameras, USB devices such as music players, and USB flashdrives for backing up files or storing items.

- **Graphics card**. This is a device that enables images, video and animations to be displayed on the laptop. It is also sometimes known as a video card. The faster the graphics card, the better the quality the relevant media will be displayed at. In general, very fast graphics cards are really only needed for intensive multimedia applications such as video games or videos.

- **Wireless**. This refers to a laptop's ability to connect wirelessly to a network – i.e. another computer or an internet connection. In order to be able to do this, the laptop must have a wireless card, which enables it to connect to a network or high-speed internet connection.

- **Ports**. These are the parts of a laptop into which external devices can be plugged, using a cable such as a USB. They are usually located on the side of the laptop, and there can be two or three of each.

- **Pointing device**. This is the part of the laptop that replaces the traditional mouse as a means of moving the cursor on the screen. Most pointing devices are in the form of a touchpad, where a finger on a pad is used to move the cursor. An external mouse can also be connected to the laptop and used in the conventional way.

- **Webcam**. This is a type of camera that is fitted into the laptop, and can be used to take still photographs or communicate via video with other people.

External optical drives can also be connected to a laptop through a USB cable.

For more on using wireless technology, see page 151.

13

USB stands for Universal Serial Bus, and is a popular way of connecting external devices to computers.

Size and Weight

The issues of size and weight are integral to the decision to buy a laptop. In addition to getting a machine with enough computing power, it is also important to ensure that the screen is large enough for your needs and that it is light enough for you to carry around comfortably.

Size

The main issue with the size of a laptop is the dimensions of the screen. This is usually measured in inches, diagonally from corner to corner. The range for the majority of laptops currently on the market is approximately 12-17 inches, with some more powerful models going up to 19 inches.

When considering the size of screen, it is important to think about how you are going to use your laptop:

- If you are going to use it mainly for functions such as letter writing and sending email, then a smaller screen might suffice.

- If you are going to use it mainly for functions such as surfing the web or editing and looking at photographs, then you may feel more comfortable with a larger screen.

- If you or anyone else is going to be using it for playing games and watching videos, then the larger the screen, the better.

Weight

Unless you are buying a laptop to replace a desktop, weight should not be too much of an issue, as most models are similar in this respect. However, make sure you physically feel the laptop before you buy it.

If you are going to be traveling a lot with your laptop, then a lighter, ultrabook type may be the best option. When considering this, take into account the weight of any type of case that you will use to carry the laptop, as this will add to the overall weight.

Beware

Looking at material on a smaller screen can be more tiring on the eyes as, by default, it is displayed proportionally smaller than on a larger screen. It is possible to change the size of the screen display, but this will lead to less material being displayed on the screen. See page 54 to view how to change the screen resolution.

Getting Comfortable

Since you will probably be using your laptop in more than one location, the issue of finding a comfortable working position can be vital, particularly as you cannot put the keyboard and monitor in different positions (as you can with a desktop computer). Whenever you are using your laptop, try to make sure that you are sitting in a comfortable position with your back well supported, and that the laptop is in a position where you can reach the keyboard easily and also see the screen without straining.

Despite the possible temptation to do so, avoid using your laptop in bed, on your lap, or where you have to slouch or strain to reach the laptop properly:

Seating position

The ideal way to sit at a laptop is with an office-type chair that offers good support for your back. Even with these types of chairs it is important to maintain a good body position so that your back is straight and your head is pointing forward.

If you do not have an office-type chair, use a chair with a straight back and place a cushion behind you for extra support and comfort, as required.

Don't forget

Working comfortably at a laptop involves a combination of a good chair, good posture and good positioning of the laptop.

Hot tip

If possible, the best place to work at a laptop is at a dedicated desk or workstation.

Hot tip

One of the advantages of office-type chairs is that the height can usually be adjusted, and this can be a great help in achieving a comfortable position.

...cont'd

Laptop position

When working at your laptop, it is important to have it positioned so that both the keyboard and the screen are in a comfortable position. If the keyboard is too low, then you will have to slouch or strain to reach it:

If the keyboard is too high, your arms will be stretching. This could lead to pain in your tendons:

The ideal setup is to have the laptop in a position where you can sit with your forearms and wrists as level as possible while you are typing on the keyboard:

Beware

Take regular breaks when working with a laptop, and stop working if you experience aches or pins and needles in your arms or legs.

Adjusting the screen

Another factor in working comfortably at a laptop is the position of the screen. Unlike with a desktop computer, it is not feasible to have a laptop screen at eye level, as this would result in the keyboard being in too high a position. Instead, once you have achieved a comfortable seating position, open the screen so that it is approximately 90 degrees from your eyeline:

Find a comfortable body position and adjust your laptop's position to this, rather than vice versa.

One problem with laptop screens is that they can reflect glare from sunlight or indoor lighting:

Most modern laptops have screens with an anti-glare coating. However, even this will not be very effective against bright sunlight that is shining directly onto the screen.

If this happens, either change your position or block out the light source, using some form of blind or shade. Avoid squinting at a screen that is reflecting glare as this will quickly give you a headache.

Carrying a Laptop

As laptops are designed for mobility, it is safe to assume that they will have to be carried around at some point. Because of the weight of even the lightest laptops, it can be uncomfortable to carry a laptop for an extended period of time. To try to minimize this, it is important to follow a few rules:

- Carry the laptop with a carry case that is designed for this task (or a double-strapped backpack).

- Carry the laptop on one side of your body and move it from side to side if necessary.

Beware

If you are carrying your laptop for a long period of time make sure that you take regular breaks, otherwise you may cause yourself a strain or an injury.

- Do not cross the strap over your shoulders, and try not to carry too many other items at the same time.

Beware

If you place your laptop with another piece of luggage, make sure that you keep it with you at all times, so as to minimize the chance of theft.

If you are traveling with your laptop you might be able to incorporate it into your luggage, particularly if it can be moved on wheels.

Keyboard and Touchpad

Laptops have the same basic data-input devices as desktop computers; i.e. a keyboard and a mouse. A laptop keyboard is very similar to a desktop one, although it is best to try the action of the keys before you buy a particular laptop, to ensure that they are not too "soft"; i.e. that there is enough resistance when they are pressed.

One of the main differences between a laptop and a desktop computer is the mouse (or pointing device) that controls the on-screen cursor. In the early days of laptops, some of them had a small control stick to move the cursor. However, these have been almost universally replaced by touchpads, which are small, sensitive, square or rectangular pads that are activated by stroking a finger over them to move the cursor. It sometimes takes a bit of practice to get used to them, but after a little experience they can be as effective as a traditional mouse. When using a keyboard or touchpad, avoid having your fingers too high:

Instead, keep your hands and fingers as flat as possible over the keyboard and the touchpad:

Don't forget

Laptop keyboards contain the same functionality as any standard computer keyboard. However, most manufacturers have keyboards with functions that are specific to their own laptops.

Using an External Mouse

Not everyone likes touchpads as a means of moving the cursor on a laptop, and it is true they can sometimes be slightly fiddly and prone to erratic movement if the control is too jerky. The good news is that it is possible to use a conventional mouse with a laptop to move the cursor.

A mouse can be connected to a laptop via one of the suitable sockets (ports) at the back or side of the laptop. These are usually in the form of USB ports:

Once the mouse has been connected to the laptop, it can be used in exactly the same way as with a desktop computer. In some cases it is possible to add a wireless mouse, which can be used without the need for a cable:

Don't forget

It is certainly worth persevering with a laptop's touchpad, even if it seems very frustrating at first. Once you have found the correct pressure to apply, it will become much easier to control.

Ports and Slots

Most laptops have a slightly bewildering array of sockets and slots for connecting external devices. These sockets are known as ports, and they come in a variety of shapes and sizes for different devices and uses:

- **USB**. This is a method for connecting a variety of external devices such as digital cameras, digital music players, scanners and printers. The latest standard in widespread use is USB 3.0, and this has largely replaced parallel and serial ports in terms of connecting devices such as printers or an external mouse.

- **USB Type-C**. This is the latest type of USB port, for devices with a USB Type-C cable. The port is thinner than a standard USB one and is reversible so that the end of the cable can be inserted both ways, rather than a single way (as for standard USB ports).

- **Ethernet**. This can be used as a cable connection to your internet router, rather than using a Wi-Fi connection.

- **HDMI (High-Definition Multimedia Interface)**. This can be used to connect to compatible digital devices, including high-definition TVs. This enables you to view whatever is on your laptop screen on a television, and is a good option for watching movies or displaying photos.

- **Memory card readers**. These are used for downloading photos from memory cards from digital cameras or smartphones. Some laptops only have an SD card slot, since these are most commonly used. If you need to attach a multi-card reader for different types of memory card, this can be done using a USB port.

The main slot on some older laptops is:

- **CD/DVD players or re-writers**. These can be used to play music CDs or watch videos on a DVD. They can also be used to copy data to blank CDs or DVDs. This is a good option for backing up items that you want to keep, such as photos.

Laptops with USB 3.0 ports can still be used with USB 2.0 (or earlier) devices, but they will also work with any USB 3.0 devices.

Not all laptops have a CD/DVD player, although external CD/DVD drives can be connected.

The Wonder of Wireless

For anyone who has struggled with a tangle of computer cables and wires, the advent of wireless technology has been one of the great computing breakthroughs of recent years.

Wireless technology does exactly what the name suggests: it allows a wireless-enabled computer to communicate with other similarly enabled devices such as other computers, printers, or an internet connection. First of all, the devices have to be set up as a network; i.e. they have to be linked together so that they know they should be communicating with each other. Once this has been done, files can be shared or sent to the printer and the internet browsed, all without the need to connect devices using a cable.

In order to be part of a wireless network, a laptop must have a wireless capability. Most modern laptops come with wireless cards already installed; otherwise, they can be installed in any available expansion slot.

Hotspots

One of the great growth areas of wireless technology is hotspots. These are public areas that have been set up to distribute the internet wirelessly. This means that anyone with a wireless card in their laptop can, if they are within a certain range, access the internet in a variety of public places. These include:

- Coffee shops
- Airports
- Hotels
- Libraries
- Supermarkets

Hotspots operate using Wi-Fi technology, which is the method by which the signal from the network is transferred to individual users. Most hotspots have a limited range of approximately 100 yards. Some are free to use, while others charge a fee, depending on usage.

Beware

One concern about hotspots is security. This is because if you can access a network wirelessly, someone else could then also access your laptop and data. Many hotspots have software in place to try to stop this.

Don't forget

For more details about Wi-Fi and networks, see Chapter 9.

Cleaning a Laptop

Like most things, laptops benefit greatly from a little care and attention. The two most important areas to keep clean are the screen and the keyboard.

Cleaning the screen

All computer screens quickly collect dust and fingerprints, and laptops are no different. If this is left too long it can make the screen harder to read, causing eye strain and headaches. Clean the screen regularly with the following cleaning materials:

- A lint-free cloth, similar to the type used to clean camera lenses (it is important not to scratch the screen in any way).

- An alcohol-free cleaning fluid that is recommended for computer screens.

- Screen wipes – again, those that are recommended for use on computer screens.

Cleaning the keyboard

Keyboards are notorious for accumulating dust, fluff and crumbs. One way to solve this problem is to turn the laptop upside down and very gently shake it to loosen any foreign objects. Failing this, a can of condensed air can be used with a narrow nozzle to blow out any stubborn items that remain lodged in the keys.

Don't forget

The outer casing of a laptop can be cleaned with the same fluid as used for the screen. Equally effective can be a duster or a damp (but not wet) cloth and warm water. Keep soap away from laptops if possible.

23

Choosing a Carry Case

When you are transporting your laptop it could be placed in any convenient bag such as a backpack, a duffle bag, or even a large handbag. However, there are several advantages to using a proper laptop carry case:

- It will probably be more comfortable when you are carrying it, as it is designed specifically for this job.

- The laptop will be more secure, as it should fit properly in the case.

- You should be able to keep all of your laptop accessories together in one case.

When choosing a carry case, look for one that fits your laptop well and has a strap to keep it secure inside:

Also, make sure that there are enough additional spaces and pockets for accessories such as cables and an external mouse. Finally, choosing a case with a padded shoulder strap will be of considerable benefit if you have to carry your laptop for any length of time.

Beware

A laptop case should also be lockable, either with its own internal lock or with a fastening through which a padlock can be put.

Spares and Accessories

Whenever you are going anywhere with your laptop, there are always spares and accessories to consider. Some of these are just nice things to have, while others could be essential to ensure that you can still use your laptop if anything goes wrong while you are on your travels. Items to consider putting in your laptop case include:

- **Spare battery**. This is probably the most important spare if you are going to be away from home for any length of time, and particularly if you think you may be unable to access a power supply for a period of time and so be unable to charge your laptop battery. Like all batteries, laptop batteries slowly lose power over time and do not keep their charge for as long as when they are new. It is a good idea to always keep an eye on how much battery power you have left and, if you are running low, try to conserve as much energy as possible. Although laptop batteries are bulky and heavy, carrying a spare could mean the difference between frustration and relief if you are left with no battery power and no charging options.

- **Power cable**. This is the cable that can be used to power the laptop when it is not being run on battery power. It usually consists of a cable and a power adapter, which makes it rather bulky and heavy. Whenever possible, this should be used rather than the internal battery, and it should be kept with the laptop at all times.

For more information on batteries, see Chapter 10.

...cont'd

Hot tip

It is important that headphones are comfortable to wear for an extended period of time. In general, the types that fit over the ears are more comfortable than the "bud" variety that is inserted into the ear.

Don't forget

Backing up (see page 181) is the process of copying folders and files from your laptop onto an external device for safekeeping in case the folders and files on the laptop are deleted or corrupted.

Beware

Most modern laptops do not have an internal DVD/CD drive, but they can be used with an external one, connected with a USB cable.

- **External mouse**. This can be used instead of the laptop's touchpad. Some people prefer a traditional mouse, particularly if they are going to be working on their laptop for an extended period of time.

- **Multi-card reader**. If you do not have a built-in multi-card reader (see page 21), an external one can be used to download photos from a digital camera memory card. This will connect via a USB port.

- **Headphones**. These can be used to listen to music or films if you are in the company of other people and you do not want to disturb them. They can also be very useful if there are distracting noises coming from other people.

- **USB flashdrive**. This is a small device that can be used to copy data to and from your laptop. It connects via a USB port and is about the size of a packet of chewing gum. It is an excellent way of backing up files from your laptop when you are away from home.

- **Cleaning material**. The materials described on page 23 can be taken to ensure your laptop is always in tip-top condition for use.

- **DVDs/CDs**. Video or music DVDs and CDs can be taken to provide mobile entertainment, and blank ones can be taken to copy data onto, similar to using a USB flashdrive.

2 Around a Laptop

This chapter shows how to quickly become familiar with your laptop and Windows 11. It gives an overview of Windows 11 so that you can become comfortable with this new environment and confidently use the Start menu, the Start button, the Taskbar, and the Desktop. It also looks at personalizing Windows 11 to exactly the way you want it.

28 **Opening Up and Turning On**

29 **Touchscreen Laptops**

30 **About Windows**

31 **Obtaining Windows 11**

32 **New Features in Windows 11**

34 **The Start Button**

36 **The Start Menu**

39 **Pinning Items**

40 **The Desktop and Taskbar**

41 **Shutting Down**

42 **Using a Microsoft Account**

44 **Personalization**

48 **Lock Screen Settings**

50 **Using Themes**

52 **Changing Color Themes**

54 **Screen Resolution**

55 **Adjusting Volume**

56 **USB Flashdrives**

Opening Up and Turning On

The first step toward getting started with a new laptop is to open it ready for use. The traditional clamshell design keeps the screen and keyboard together through the use of an internal clip or connector. This can be released by a button on the exterior of the laptop, which is usually positioned at the front or side. Some laptops have a magnetic connection between the screen and the main body.

Beware

Open the screen of your laptop carefully, so as not to put any unnecessary pressure on the connection between the screen and the main body of the laptop.

Once the screen has been opened, it can then be positioned ready for use. The screen should stay in any position in which it is placed:

Beware

Press the **Power** button with one firm, definite motion. If you accidentally press it twice in quick succession, the laptop may turn on and then shut down immediately afterward.

The **Power** button for turning on a laptop, ready for use, is usually located near to the keyboard:

The laptop can be turned on by pushing this button firmly. The laptop will then probably make a sound, to indicate that it has been turned on, and begin loading the operating system (the software that is used to run and manage all of the laptop's apps, folders and files). Once the laptop has completed its startup procedure, the opening screen should be displayed. At this point, the laptop is ready for use.

Don't forget

Most laptops will take a couple of minutes to start up and be fully ready to use.

Touchscreen Laptops

Windows 11 is the latest operating system from Microsoft, and this will be installed on most new laptops. It is optimized for touchscreen use, so it is ideal for using with laptops with touchscreen capability and also with Windows 11 tablets.

Touchscreen laptops still have a traditional keyboard but navigation can also be done by tapping, swiping and pinching on the screen. Some of the functions that can be performed on a touchscreen laptop are:

- Activate a button, such as **Done** or **OK**, by tapping on it. Apps on the Windows 11 interface can also be accessed by tapping on them from the Start menu.

- Move up and down long pages by swiping in the required direction; e.g. to navigate around web pages.

- Zoom in and out of pages by pinching inward or outward with thumb and forefinger (if the open app has this functionality). It is most commonly used for zooming in and out of web pages.

Touchscreen laptops are a realistic option for users who want to get the most out of the functionality of Windows 11. Some laptop manufacturers to look at are:

- Acer
- Dell
- HP
- Lenovo
- Sony
- Toshiba

A number of touchscreen models can also be converted into tablet mode, either by revolving the screen or by detaching the keyboard. There are also some hybrid models with a detachable screen that can be used as either a tablet or a traditional laptop with the keyboard attached.

Windows 11 was released in October 2021. This is the latest version of Windows.

The Microsoft Surface Pro tablet also runs on Windows 11, and it is a realistic option in terms of replacing a regular laptop.

About Windows

Windows is an operating system made by Microsoft, for PCs (personal computers), laptops and tablets. The operating system is the software that organizes and controls all of the components (hardware and software) in your computer.

The first operating system from Microsoft was known as MS-DOS (Microsoft Disk Operating System). This was a non-graphical, line-oriented, command-driven operating system, able to run only one application at a time. The original Windows system was an interface manager that ran on top of the MS-DOS system, providing a graphical user interface (GUI) and using clever processor and memory management to allow it to run more than one application or function at a time.

The basic element of Windows was its "windowing" capability. A window (with a lowercase "w") is a rectangular area used to display information or to run a program or app. Several windows can be opened at the same time so that you can work with multiple applications. This provided a dramatic increase in productivity, in comparison with the original MS-DOS.

Between 1985 and 2015 Microsoft released numerous versions of the operating system, each with its own intermediate versions to add updates and security fixes to the operating system. These versions of Windows included Windows 95, Windows 8 and Windows 10 (there was no Windows 9).

For several years, Microsoft stated that there would not be a full naming update to Windows 10; instead, it would continue with incremental updates, usually on an annual basis. However, nothing stays still in the world of technology and Windows 11 was released in October 2021, recognizing the fact that the operating system required a major update to keep it at the forefront of the evolution of PCs and laptops, and also mobile devices such as the Surface tablet. Windows 11 is a full redesign of the operating system, in terms of its overall appearance, and Microsoft has also taken the opportunity to add a range of new features and functions.

Obtaining Windows 11

Windows 11 is an online service, rather than just a stand-alone operating system. This means that by default, Windows 11 is obtained and downloaded online, with subsequent updates and upgrades also provided online.

The main ways of installing Windows 11 are:

- **Use Windows Update** – Replace an older version of Windows, retaining the installed applications and settings. This can be done through the **Settings** app (select **Windows Update** and click on the **Check for updates** button).

- **Microsoft website** – Visit the software download page on the

  Microsoft website (**microsoft.com/en-us/software-download/windows11**) to use the **Windows 11 Installation Assistant** to download Windows 11.

- **Pre-installed** – Buy a new laptop with Windows 11 already installed.

Some of the steps that the installation will go through are:

- **Personalize**. These are settings that will be applied to your version of Windows 11. These settings can also be selected within the Settings app once Windows 11 has been installed.

- **Settings**. You can choose to have express settings applied or customize them.

- **Microsoft Account**. You can set up a Microsoft Account during installation, or once you have started Windows.

- **Privacy**. Certain privacy settings can be applied during the setup process for Windows 11.

For more information about the Settings app, see pages 60-61.

These features are new or updated in Windows 11.

The color of the Start menu and the Taskbar below it can be set to Light or Dark. To do this, select **Settings** > **Personalization** > **Colors** and select **Light** or **Dark** in the **Choose your mode** section. The color of the Start menu and the Taskbar are a matter of personal taste (although the **Dark** option can make items clearer). The majority of the examples in the book use the **Dark** option.

New Features in Windows 11

Windows 11 is a significant update to its predecessor in terms of look and feel and also has a range of new functionality. However, it retains the features that will be familiar to Windows users, ensuring that Windows 11 is a sleek, efficient, modern operating system for Windows users.

Redesigned interface

The first obvious change with Windows 11 is a cleaner, brighter user interface, starting with the Desktop.

Updated Start button and Start menu

Two of the most important elements of Windows have been redesigned in Windows 11: the Start button, which has always been in the bottom left-hand corner, now takes up a more central position, with the Taskbar centered on the screen rather than stretching all the way across it; and the Start menu has been completely redesigned to make it easier to find apps and files.

Widgets

The Widgets app is a customizable panel that can be used to display a range of real-time information, such as newsfeeds and weather forecasts, accessed from this icon on the Taskbar. —————————————

Don't forget

There are no specific settings for the Widgets app, but there is a **Manage interests** option for determining what appears within the app. This can be accessed from the **Account** button in the top right-hand corner of the widgets panel.

Microsoft Teams Chat

Microsoft Teams is a collaboration and communication app. The full version is included with Windows 11, pinned to the Taskbar, and there is also a pop-out Teams **Chat** app that can be used independently of the full version for text, video and audio chats, accessed from this icon on the Taskbar. —————————————

Hot tip

Click on the **Add widgets** button in the main widgets panel to access options for adding a range of new widgets to the panel.

Add widgets

The Start Button

The Start button has been a significant part of Windows computing for numerous versions of the operating system. There have been various changes to the Start button over the years and it has again been redesigned in Windows 11, with the main difference being that it occupies a more central position on the screen, as opposed to being located in the left-hand corner.

Using the Start button

The Start button provides access to the apps on your Windows 11 laptop and also to the enhanced Start menu.

The Start button has been updated in Windows 11.

1 Click on the **Start** button at the bottom left-hand side of the Taskbar

Items on the Start menu can be customized from the **Personalization** > **Start** section of the Settings app.

2 The **Start** menu is displayed

Click on the **Power** button on the Start menu to access options for **Sleep**, **Shut down** or **Restart**.

3 The Start menu contains access to all of the apps on your laptop, and also recommended items

4 Other items can also be accessed from the Start button by right-clicking on it; see the next page

Power User menu

In addition to accessing the Start menu, the Start button also provides access to the Power User menu, which can be accessed as follows:

1 Right-click on the **Start** button to view the Power User menu

2 Click on the relevant buttons to view items including the **Desktop** and other popular locations such as **File Explorer**

Apps and Features
Mobility Center
Power Options
Event Viewer
System
Device Manager
Network Connections
Disk Management
Computer Management
Windows Terminal
Windows Terminal (Admin)
Task Manager
Settings
File Explorer
Search
Run
Shut down or sign out   >
Desktop

The Start button Power User menu in Step 1 has a number of options for accessing system functions, such as **Device Manager** and **Disk Management**. The options vary depending on the type of device being used.

35

3 Right-click on the Start button to access **Shut down or sign out** options (see page 41)

Settings   Sign out
File Explorer   Sleep
Search   Update and shut down
Run   Shut down
Shut down or sign out   >   Update and restart
Desktop   Restart

The Start Menu

The Start menu has been updated in Windows 11.

The Start menu has been a permanent fixture in Windows, but its appearance and functionality have changed significantly over the years. This evolution continues with Windows 11, with a newly designed Start menu. This is where you can access areas within your laptop, perform certain functions, and also access apps from a variety of locations. To use the Start menu:

1 Click on the **Start button** to access the **Start menu**. **Pinned** apps (see page 39) are shown at the top of the Start menu, with **Recommended** items below. Click on an item to open it

Hot tip

The options in Step 3 can also be accessed by right-clicking on the Start button and clicking on the **Shut down or sign out** button.

2 Click here to access your own account settings or sign out from your account

3 Click on the **Power** button for options to **Sleep** your laptop, **Shut down** or **Restart**

4 Click on the **All apps** button at the top of the **Pinned** section, to view all of the apps on your laptop

Hot tip

Scroll up and down on the **Pinned** section to view more items, or click on these buttons at the right-hand side of the Pinned section:

5 Scroll up and down the **All apps** section to view the available apps. Click on one to open it

Don't forget

At the top of the **All apps** window is a list of your **Most used** apps.

6 Click on the **Back** button in the top right-hand corner of the All apps panel to go back to the main Start menu

...cont'd

7 On the **All apps** screen, click on one of the alphabetic headings; e.g. B

Hot tip

Use the Search box at the top of the Start menu to search for specific apps.

8 An alphabetic grid is displayed

9 Click on a character on the alphabetic grid to go to the relevant section

Pinning Items

In most cases, you will want to have quick access to a variety of apps on the Start menu, not just the Windows 11 apps. It is possible to "pin" any app to the Start menu so that it is always readily available. To do this:

1 Access the alphabetical list of apps, from the Start button

Apps can be unpinned from the Start menu by right-clicking on them and selecting **Unpin from Start** from the menu that appears.

39

2 Right-click on an app and click on the **Pin to Start** button

3 The app is pinned to the Start menu

Apps can be pinned to the Taskbar in a similar way as for pinning them to the Start menu. To do this, right-click on an app and click on **More** > **Pin to taskbar**.

The Desktop and Taskbar

The Desktop is an integral part of Windows, and when you turn on Windows 11 it opens at the Desktop. This also displays the Taskbar at the bottom of the screen:

Shortcut icons   Desktop background

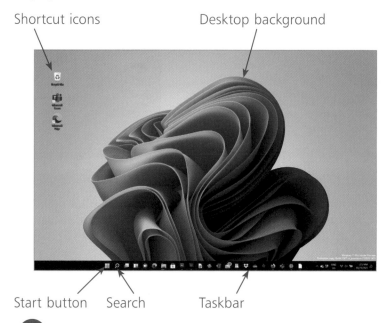

Start button   Search   Taskbar

1. Move the cursor over items on the Taskbar to see open windows for that item. Click on a window to make that the active one

2. The Notifications area at the right-hand side of the Taskbar has speaker, network and other system tools. Click on one to see more information about that item

Shutting Down

Options for shutting down Windows have been amended with some versions of the operating system. In Windows 11, this functionality can be accessed from the Start menu or the Start button.

Shutting down from the Start menu

1 Click on the **Start** button

2 Click on the **Power** button

3 Click on either the **Sleep**, **Shut down** or **Restart** buttons; or

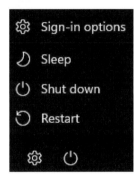

For some updates to Windows, you will need to restart your laptop for them to take effect.

Shutting down from the Start button

1 Right-click on the **Start** button and select either **Sign out**, **Sleep**, **Shut down** or **Restart** from the **Shut down or sign out** option

Using a Microsoft Account

We live in a world of ever-increasing computer connectivity, where users expect to be able to access their content wherever they are and share it with their friends and family. This is known as cloud computing, with content being stored on online servers, from where it can be accessed by authorized users with the appropriate account. In Windows 11, this type of connectivity is achieved with a Microsoft Account. This is a registration system that provides access to a number of services via the Windows 11 apps, including:

Beware

Without a Microsoft Account you will not be able to access the full functionality of the apps listed here.

- **Mail**. This is the Windows 11 email app that can be used to access and manage your different email accounts.

- **Teams**. This is the Windows collaboration and communication app.

- **People**. This is the address book app, accessed from the Mail app (above).

- **Calendar**. This is the calendar and organizer app.

- **Microsoft Store**. This is the online store for previewing and downloading additional apps.

- **OneDrive**. This is the online backup and sharing option.

Creating a Microsoft Account

It is free to create a Microsoft Account. This can be done with an email address and, together with a password, provides a unique identifier for logging in to your Microsoft Account and related apps. There are several ways to do this:

- During the initial setup process when you install Windows 11. If you do not create an account at this point, you can always do so at a later time.

- When you first open an app that requires access to a Microsoft Account. When you do this, you will be prompted to create a new account.

- From the **Accounts** section of the **Settings** app (see page 61).

Whichever way you use to create a Microsoft Account, the process is similar.

1 When you are first prompted to sign in with a Microsoft Account you can enter your account details, if you have one; or

2 Click on the **No account? Create one!** link

Microsoft Account details can also be used as your sign-in for Windows 11 (see pages 58-59).

43

3 Enter your name, an email address and a password (on the next screen) for your Microsoft Account

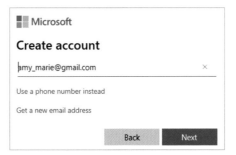

4 Click on the **Next** button to move through the registration process

Next

5 A verification code is required to finish setting up the Microsoft Account. This will be sent to the email address entered in Step 3. Click on the **Next** button to complete the Microsoft Account setup

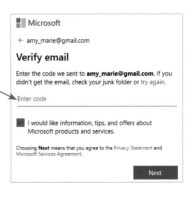

Personalization

Customizing the look and feel of Windows 11 is a good way to make it feel like it is your own personal device. This can be done with some of the options in the Personalization section of the Settings app. This includes customizing the Desktop background.

Don't forget

For more details about using the Settings app, see pages 60-61.

Don't forget

Click in the **Personalize your background** section in Step 2 and select an option for the background, from **Picture**, **Solid color** or **Slideshow**.

1 Open the **Settings** app and click on the **Personalization** tab

2 Click on the **Background** option to select a new Desktop background

3 The image selected in Step 2 becomes the Desktop background

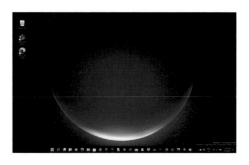

44

4 To select one of your own pictures for the Desktop background, click on the **Browse photos** button next to the **Choose a photo** option

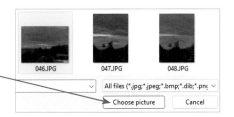

5 Browse to the required photo, select it, and click on the **Choose picture** button

6 The photo is added to the **Background** section of the Personalization settings, and remains available here even if another background is selected

Click in the **Choose a fit for your desktop image** box to specify how the picture fills the background screen. The options are: **Fill**, **Fit**, **Stretch**, **Tile**, **Center**, and **Span**.

7 The photo is added as the Desktop background

...cont'd

Personalizing colors

Many of the color elements of Windows 11 can also be personalized. To do this:

1 Within the **Personalization** settings, click on the **Colors** option

2 The color personalization options are displayed within the main Colors window

The **Light** and **Dark** options in Step 4 are applied to the Taskbar and the Start menu.

3 For the **Choose your mode** option, click here

4 Select an option for the colors for the Windows 11 interface, from **Light**, **Dark**, or **Custom**

Light

Dark

| Custom

5 The same color options as in Step 4 can also be selected for the **Choose your default Windows mode** and **Choose your default app mode** options

Choose your default Windows mode

Choose your default app mode

46

6 Drag the **Transparency effects** button **On** to enable the background behind a window to show through it to a certain degree

7 Turn the **Show accent color on Start and taskbar** and **Show accent color on title bars and windows borders** options **On** or **Off**, as required

Hot tip

If the **Transparency effects** button is **On**, the colors behind a window will change as the window is moved around the screen.

8 To select your own colors for accent colors, click on the **Accent color** section and select the **Manual** option

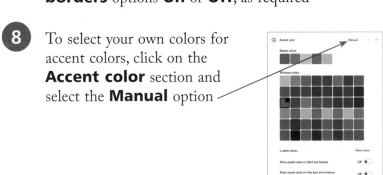

9 Click on the **View colors** button

10 Click on an area of the color chart to select a new color and click on the **Done** button

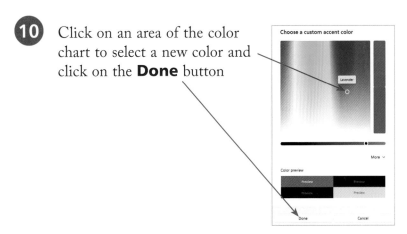

47

Lock Screen Settings

The Settings app enables you to set the appearance of the Lock screen and the Start menu, and to select an account photo. To do this, first access the settings.

1 Open the **Settings** app and click on the **Personalization** tab

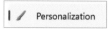

2 Click on the **Lock screen** option

3 The current Lock screen background is shown here

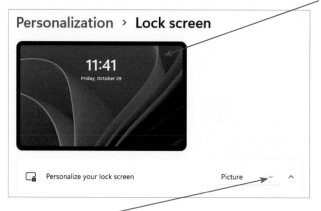

4 Click here to select options for the Lock screen background

5 Select one of the Lock screen background options from **Windows spotlight**, **Picture** or **Slideshow**

Don't forget

If **Slideshow** is selected in Step 5, you will then have the option to choose an album of photos to use as a slideshow for the Lock screen background.

6 For the **Picture** option, click on the
Browse photos button to select your own picture

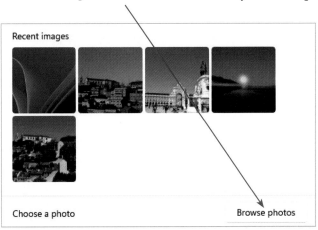

7 Select an
image and
click on
**Choose
picture** to
add this to the
background
options for the
Lock screen

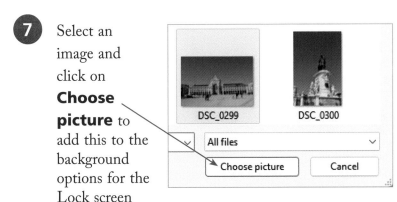

Hot tip

If you use your own
images for the Lock
screen background,
these will remain
available on the
thumbnail row even
if you switch to
another image for the
background.

8 Other options for the Lock screen include selecting
apps that display their detailed status on the Lock
screen, and showing the Lock screen background
image on the sign-in screen, as well as the Lock
screen

49

Using Themes

Themes in Windows 11 can be used to customize several items for the look and feel of Windows.

1 Open **Settings** and click on the **Personalization** tab

2 Click on the **Themes** option

3 The current theme is displayed

The preset themes in Step 5 combine all of the elements in Step 4 that can be used to customize a theme.

4 Make a selection for a customized theme, using **Background**, **Color**, **Sounds** and **Mouse cursor**

5 The selections for the customized theme are shown in the **Current theme** preview window

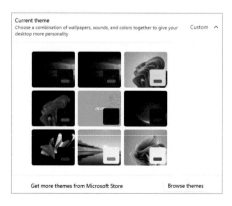

6 Click on the **Save** button to use it for the current theme

7 Click on one of the preset themes to select it rather than customizing one

8 Elements of the preset theme are displayed in the preview window

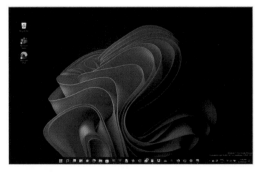

An internet connection is required to download more themes from the Microsoft Store.

9 Click on the **Browse themes** button in the **Get more themes from Microsoft Store** section to download more themes that can be used on your laptop

Changing Color Themes

The Colors option in the Personalization section of the Settings app can be used to edit the overall color scheme of Windows 11, including a Light theme that applies a crisper look and feel to all elements of the Windows 11 interface. To create this:

The color themes do not alter the Desktop background. This is done in **Settings** > **Personalization** > **Background**.

1 Open the **Settings** app and click on the **Personalization** tab

2 Click on the **Colors** option

3 Click the drop-down menu in the **Choose your mode** section

4 Click on the **Light** option to apply a Light theme to the elements of Windows 11

5 The Light theme is also applied to the Start menu and the Taskbar

6 If the **Dark** option is selected in Step 4 on the previous page, the background and foreground will be inverted

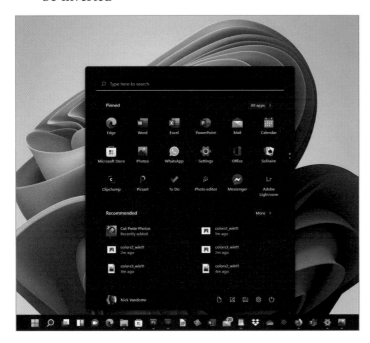

7 Click the drop-down menus in the **Choose your default Windows mode** section and the **Choose your default app mode** section to select specific settings. For instance, the Windows mode could be **Dark**, and the default app mode could be **Light**

The Dark theme for apps can be useful in the evening, or in low-level lighting, as it can be more relaxing on the eyes when looking at content on the screen.

Screen Resolution

If you have a high-resolution screen, you may find that the text, as well as the icons, is too small. You can increase the effective size by reducing the screen resolution.

1 Open the **Settings** app (see the next page), select **System** and then click on the **Display** option

Display
Monitors, brightness, night light, display profile

2 Click here to change the screen resolution. Select a new resolution value from the list

Display resolution
Adjust the resolution to fit your connected display

1680 × 1050 (Recommended) ∨

3 Click on a screen resolution, as required

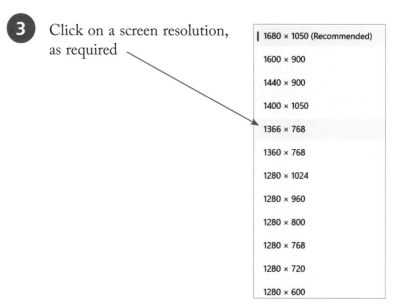

1680 × 1050 (Recommended)

1600 × 900

1440 × 900

1400 × 1050

1366 × 768

1360 × 768

1280 × 1024

1280 × 960

1280 × 800

1280 × 768

1280 × 720

1280 × 600

4 Click on the **Keep changes** button to change the screen resolution

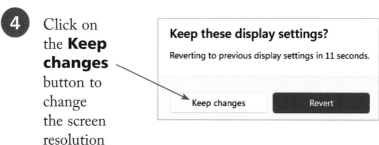

Keep these display settings?

Reverting to previous display settings in 11 seconds.

Keep changes   Revert

Adjusting Volume

In Windows 11, the sound options for adjusting the volume for a laptop can be selected in the Settings app. To do this:

1 Click on the **Settings** app on the Taskbar, or from the Start menu

2 Click on the **System** tab System

3 Click on the **Sound** button

4 In the Sound section, click here to choose the speakers to use and drag this slider to specify the volume

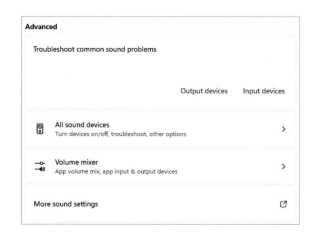

5 Scroll down the page to view the **Advanced** sound options, including those for all of the available devices and for mixing volumes

55

Beware

If you are going to be using your laptop near other people and without headphones, make sure the volume controls are set at a reasonable level, so as not to annoy people.

Hot tip

You can adjust the volume of your laptop's speakers, or mute them, by clicking on this icon in the Notifications area at the right-hand side of the Taskbar:

USB Flashdrives

USB flashdrives are small devices that can be used for copying files and then transferring them between computers. To connect a flashdrive to a laptop and use it:

1 Connect the flashdrive to one of the laptop's USB ports

2 The flashdrive should be recognized automatically and the necessary software installed so that it is ready to use

3 Access the Desktop and click on the **File Explorer** button on the Taskbar

4 The flashdrive should appear as a removable drive under **This PC**. (Flashdrives can be renamed in File Explorer by right-clicking on the name and selecting **Rename**)

5 Double-click on the flashdrive to view its contents. The files can then be used in the same way as any others on your laptop

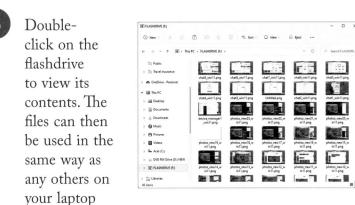

3

Getting Up and Running

This chapter looks at some of the features of Windows 11, including the settings and using the search facility Cortana. It also shows how to access and use File Explorer.

58 Sign-in Options

60 Settings

62 Searching

64 Setting Up Cortana

65 Using Cortana

68 Viewing Notifications

70 Opening File Explorer

71 Quick Access in File Explorer

73 File Explorer Menu Bar

Sign-in Options

Each time you start up your laptop using Windows 11 with a Microsoft Account, you will need to sign in. This is a security feature so that no-one can gain unauthorized access to your account on your laptop. The sign-in process starts with the Lock screen, and then you have to enter your sign-in details.

1. When you start your laptop, the **Lock screen** will be showing. This is linked to the **Sign-in screen**

2. Click on the **Lock screen** or press any key to move to the **Sign-in** screen. Enter your sign-in details and press **Enter** on your keyboard

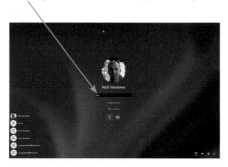

3. On the **Sign-in screen**, click on this button to select **Accessibility** options

4. On the **Sign-in screen**, click on this button to select **Power off** options including **Shut down**, **Sleep** and **Restart**

5 If there are other users with an account on the same laptop, their names will be displayed here

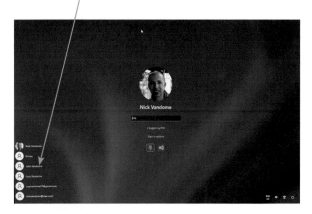

6 Click on another user to access their own **Sign-in screen**

Sign-in settings

Settings for how you sign in can be accessed from the Accounts section in the Settings app.

1 Access the **Settings** app and click on the **Accounts** button

Accounts

2 Under **Sign-in options**, select options for how you sign in from the **Lock screen**

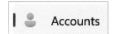

You can sign in with a Local Account or a Microsoft Account. If you sign in with the latter, you will have access to related services, such as Mail and People. Also, you will be able to sync your settings and use them on another computer when you log in with your account.

For details about using the Settings app, see pages 60-61.

Facial recognition and **Fingerprint recognition** are functions that use biometric authentication for signing in to Windows 11. Both of them require appropriate hardware devices.

Some of the settings have been updated in Windows 11.

Add the **Settings** app to the Taskbar for quick access. To do this, access it from the Start menu, right-click on it and click on **More** > **Pin to taskbar**.

Click here on the Taskbar to access the Quick Settings panel containing the most frequently used settings. Click on this button to edit the items in the Quick Settings panel:

Settings

Accessing the Settings app

The Settings app in Windows 11 provides options for how you set up your laptop and how it operates. There are 11 main Settings categories, each of which has a number of sub-categories. To access and use the Settings app:

1 Click on the **Start** button

2 Click on the **Settings** button on the Start menu; or

3 Click on the **Settings** button on the Taskbar

In the **Settings** app, click on one of the main categories in the left-hand navigation panel to view options within that category, in the main window.

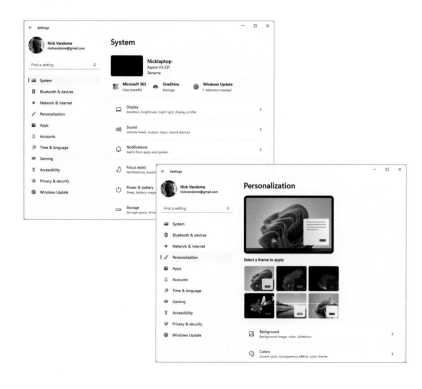

Settings categories

The main categories in the Settings app all contain a range of options for customizing the way that Windows 11 looks and operates, and they are:

- **System**. These are settings for how your laptop operates, including options for the display, notifications, power and sleep, and battery and storage.

- **Bluetooth & devices**. These are settings for how devices connect to your laptop, including Bluetooth devices, printers, touchpad and USB devices.

- **Network & internet**. These are settings for connecting to networks, including connecting to the internet by Wi-Fi, Ethernet cable or dial-up modem.

- **Personalization**. These are settings for personalizing a range of options for your laptop, including background, colors, Lock screen, themes, Start menu and the Taskbar.

- **Apps**. These are settings for managing your apps, including viewing details and setting default apps.

- **Accounts**. These are settings for viewing and changing account settings and also setting up new accounts.

- **Time & language**. These are settings for the time, language and region used on your laptop.

- **Gaming**. These are settings for managing gamer options, including activating Game Mode and using the Game Bar.

- **Accessibility**. These are settings for accessibility options, covering sight and hearing issues.

- **Privacy and security**. These are settings for general privacy options and also location settings for apps using your location.

- **Windows Update**. These are settings for updating Windows and a range of security options.

Computer screens emit a blue light that can be disruptive in terms of maintaining good sleeping routines at night. The amount of blue light can be decreased in the evening, in the **System** > **Display** settings. Click on the **Night light** button in the main panel and apply the required settings (the default is to enable the Night light settings from **Sunset to sunrise**).

System text can be made bigger within **Accessibility** > **Text size** by dragging the **Text size** slider. Click on the **Apply** button to apply any changes.

Searching

Searching for items and information on computers and the internet has come a long way since the first search engines on the web. Most computer operating systems now have sophisticated search facilities for finding things on your own computer as well as searching over the web. They also now have personal digital assistants, which are voice-activated search functions that can be used instead of typing search requests.

Windows 11 has a Search icon built into the Taskbar. Separate searches can be performed with Cortana, the digital voice assistant (see pages 64-67).

Using the Search box for text searching

To use the Search box for text-only searches, over either your laptop or the web:

Hot tip

The top search result (**Best match**) is displayed at the top of the window in Step 3.

Hot tip

Click on the buttons at the top of the Search window to specify locations over which the search will be performed. These are **All**, **Apps**, **Documents**, **Web** and **More**.

1 Click on this button on the Taskbar

2 The Search box is at the top of the window

3 Enter a search term (or website address)

4 Click on one of the results, or on one of the **See web results** buttons, to view the search results page in the Microsoft Edge browser

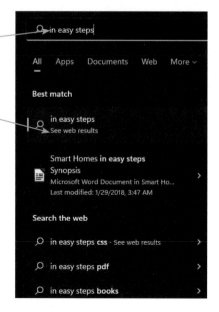

Asking a question

The Search box can also be used to ask specific questions.

1 Enter a question in the Search box

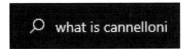

2 Click on the **See web results** button at the top of the Search box to view the results in the Microsoft Edge browser

The magnifying glass icon indicates that a search is going to be undertaken on the web, and this will be displayed on a search results page, as in Step 2.

Searching over your laptop

As well as searching over the web, the Search box can also be used to find items on your laptop.

1 Enter a search query in the Search box and click on one of the options on the top toolbar to search for items from that location on your laptop; e.g. Documents. Click on one of the results to open the item on your laptop

If you are searching for a keyword over files on your laptop, the search will be conducted over the text in documents and folders, not just the document titles. It will also search over the online backup and storage facility, OneDrive, if you have this set up (see pages 110-113).

Setting Up Cortana

To ensure that you can use Cortana to perform voice searches and queries, the language settings on your Windows 11 laptop have to be set up correctly. To do this:

The country or region, display language and speech language should be the same in order for Cortana to work.

1 Open the **Settings** app and click on the **Time & language** tab

2 Click on the **Language & region** option

🌐 Language & region
Windows and some apps format dates and time based on your region

3 Click here to select a country or region

Region

🌐 Country or region
Windows and apps might use your country or region to give you local content
United States ⌄

🌐 Regional format
Windows and some apps format dates and times based on your regional format
ⓘ Some apps may need to be closed and reopened to see formatting changes.
English (United States) ⌄   ⌄

4 Select a **Regional format**, which should match the region in Step 3

Once Cortana has been set up, it can be accessed from this icon on the Start menu, and it can also be pinned to the Start menu and the Taskbar – see page 39 for details.

⭕ Cortana

5 Click on the **Speech** option under **Time & language**

🕬 Speech
Speech language, speech recognition microphone setup, voices

6 Select the same **Speech language** as the one used as the display language in Step 4

Speech language

Choose the language you speak with your device

English (United States) ⌄

Using Cortana

Voice searching with Cortana

As with text searches, Cortana can be used to search over various places and for different items.

Open the Cortana app from the Start menu to begin your voice search. The Cortana app can also be pinned to the Taskbar (see page 39).

1 Click on the **Microphone** button to the right of the Cortana box to begin a voice search

2 This symbol is displayed in the Search window to indicate that Cortana is listening

3 Cortana can be used for a wide range of general voice requests, which display results from the web; e.g. ask about the capital city of a country and click on the result to see more details on the web

Cortana can be used directly from the Lock screen to ask general queries such as "What is the weather in my area?" or to play a song from the Groove Music app.

4 Queries can also be made in relation to the web; e.g. opening a specific

website. Cortana can also be used to display specific information from the web, such as a weather forecast or sports results

...cont'd

5 If the query is general – e.g. "**Open Microsoft**" – various options in terms of apps from your laptop will be displayed. Click on one of the apps to open it directly from Cortana

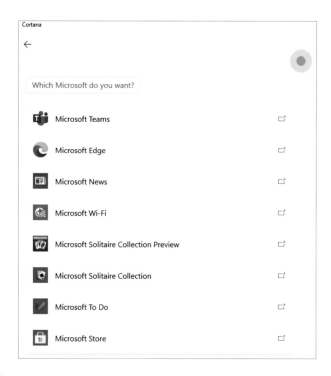

Don't forget

Cortana voice commands can be used to turn off, restart or put your laptop to sleep. They can also be used to change the system volume. Also, an increasing range of apps support Cortana, so can be used in conjunction with it; e.g. for playing movies with Netflix.

6 Cortana can be used to open specific apps; e.g. by saying "**Open Microsoft Edge**". If required, options will be available, depending on the request. Click on an item to access it

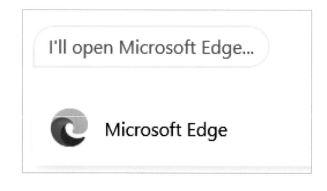

Cortana settings

A range of settings can be made for Cortana directly from the Cortana window when a search is being performed.

1 Open Cortana and click on the **Menu** button in the top left-hand corner of the Cortana window

2 Click on the **Settings** option

3 The Cortana settings are displayed

4 Click on the **Privacy** button in Step 3 to access options for specifying information Cortana can store about you, and how to clear data

5 Click on the **Microphone** button in Step 3 to access options to specify permissions for the microphone and also for setting up **Voice activation**, for starting a Cortana search by saying "**Cortana**"

Viewing Notifications

In the modern digital world, there is an increasing desire to keep updated about what is happening in our online world. With Windows 11, the Notifications area can be used to display information from a variety of sources so that you never miss an update or a notification from one of your apps. To view your notifications:

Click on a notification to open it and view its full contents.

1 Click here at the far right of the Taskbar. The number of new notifications is displayed

Notifications for certain apps also appear on screen for a short period of time in a small banner, to alert you to the fact that there is a new notification.

2 Notifications are displayed in the Notifications panel. Click on a notification to open it and view its full contents

3 Click on the **Clear all** button to remove all current notifications

The Focus assist settings can also be accessed from **Settings** > **System** > **Notifications**, and click on the **Focus assist** option for a range of options for selecting times for when notifications are silenced.

4 Click on the **Focus assist settings** option, at the top of the Notifications panel, to apply settings when notifications are not active

...cont'd

Settings for notifications

To change settings for notifications:

1 Click on the **Settings** app and click on the **System** tab

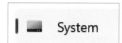

2 Click on the **Notifications** option

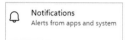

3 Drag the **Notifications** button **On**. Under the **Notifications from apps and senders** heading, drag the buttons **On** or **Off** to specify items that appear in the Notifications panel. For instance, if the **Mail** button is **On**, you will be notified whenever you receive a new email

4 Click on an app to specify how notifications operate for it. Options include showing banners on the screen when a notification arrives, and also for playing a sound – or not – for a notification

Notifications can also be shown on the Lock screen by clicking on the down-pointing arrow next to the **Notifications** option and checking the **Show notifications on the lock screen** checkbox **On**.

Opening File Explorer

Although File Explorer is not necessarily one of the first apps that you will use with Windows 11, it still plays an important role in organizing your folders and files. To access File Explorer:

1 From the Desktop, click on this icon on the Taskbar; or

Some shortcuts in Windows 11 are accessed together with the **WinKey** (**Windows key**) on the keyboard:

2 Press **WinKey** + **E**, and File Explorer opens at the **Quick access** folder

3 When File Explorer is opened, click on the **This PC** option to view the top-level items on your laptop, including the main folders, your hard drive and any removable devices that are connected

This PC displays files from different locations as a single collection, without actually moving any files.

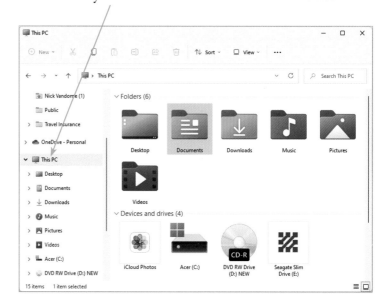

Quick Access in File Explorer

When working with files and folders, there will probably be items that you access on a regular basis. The Quick access section of File Explorer can be used to view the items that you have most recently accessed, and also to pin your most frequently used and favorite items. To use the Quick access section:

1 Click on the right-pointing arrow on the **Quick access** button in the File Explorer Navigation pane so that it becomes downward-pointing

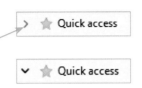

Items displayed under Quick access are not physically located there; the links are just shortcuts to the actual location within your file structure.

2 In the main window, your frequently used folders and most recently used files are displayed

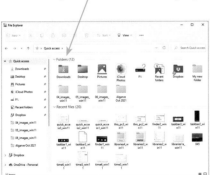

3 The folders are also listed underneath the **Quick access** button in the Navigation pane

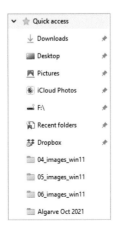

...cont'd

Adding items to Quick access
The folders that you access and use most frequently can be pinned to the Quick access section. This does not physically move them; it just creates a shortcut within Quick access. To do this:

To unpin an item from Quick access, right-click on it and click on **Unpin from Quick access**.

1 Right-click on the folder you want to pin, and click on **Pin to Quick access**

2 The folder is pinned to the Quick access section, which is denoted by the pin symbol; or

3 Drag the folder over the **Quick access** button until the **Pin to Quick access** option appears, and release

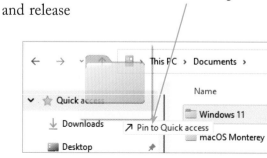

File Explorer Menu Bar

The Menu bar in File Explorer has been simplified in Windows 11, replacing the Scenic Ribbon, but it can still be used for a variety of tasks for viewing and managing items within File Explorer.

1 The Menu bar is displayed at the top of File Explorer, regardless of which window is being viewed. If nothing is selected in File Explorer, a number of options are unavailable (grayed out)

2 Click on an item within a File Explorer window to activate more of the options on the Menu bar

3 Click on the down-pointing arrow next to an item in the Menu bar to access its additional options

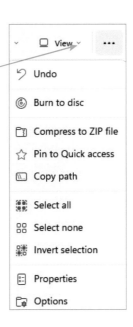

The File Explorer Menu bar has been updated in Windows 11.

Hot tip

Hover your mouse over the buttons to see the button names.

Don't forget

Right-click anywhere within a File Explorer window to access the File Explorer context menu; i.e. one that applies to the item in the current window.

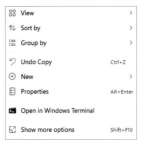

...cont'd

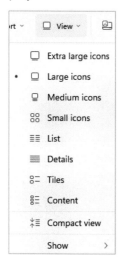

Click on the **View** button on the File Explorer Menu bar to select options for how the items in a File Explorer window are displayed.

④ Click on the **New** button to view options for creating new files with specific apps, and also new folders and shortcuts to items within File Explorer

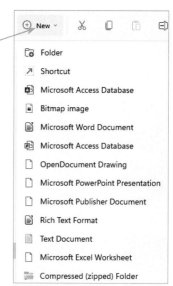

⑤ Depending on the content of a folder, different options are displayed on the Menu bar; e.g. if photos are selected, there are options specific to managing these

⑥ Select an item in a File Explorer window and click on the **Share** button to access options for sharing the selected item with other people, using email, social media, or online storage services

4 Working with Apps

In Windows 11, some apps are pre-installed, while hundreds more can be downloaded from the Microsoft Store. This chapter shows how to work with and organize apps.

76 Starting with Apps

78 Windows 11 Apps

80 Using Windows 11 Apps

82 Closing Apps

83 Searching for Apps

84 Using the Microsoft Store

87 Buying Apps

88 Viewing Your Apps

89 Installing and Uninstalling Apps

Starting with Apps

The word "app" is now firmly established as a generic term for computer programs on a range of devices. Originally, apps were items that were downloaded to smartphones and tablet computers. However, the terminology has now been expanded to cover any computer program. So, in Windows 11 most programs are referred to as "apps", although some legacy ones may still be referred to as "programs".

There are three main types of apps within Windows 11:

- **Windows 11 apps**. These are built-in apps that can be accessed from the Start menu. They cover the areas of communication, entertainment and information, and several of them are linked together through the online sharing service, OneDrive. In Windows 11, they open in their own window on the Desktop, in the same way as the older-style Windows apps (see below).

- **Windows classic apps**. These are older-style Windows apps that people may be familiar with from previous versions of Windows. These open in the Desktop environment.

- **Microsoft Store apps**. These are apps that can be downloaded from the online Microsoft Store and cover a wide range of subjects and functionality. Some Microsoft Store apps are free, while others have to be paid for.

In Windows 11, all apps open directly on the Desktop and their operation is more consistent, regardless of the type of app.

Apps for use with Android devices can also be downloaded from the Microsoft Store so that they can be synchronized with the same app on your Android devices. To find these, enter **"android apps"** into the Search box at the top of the Microsoft Store window. This is a new feature in Windows 11.

Windows 11 apps
Windows 11 apps are accessed from the icons on the Start menu. Click on a tile to open the relevant app.

Windows classic apps
Windows classic apps are generally the ones that appeared as default with previous versions of Windows, and would have been accessed from the Start button. Windows classic apps can be accessed from the Start menu by using the alphabetic list, or searched for via the Taskbar Search box. Windows classic apps have the traditional Windows look and functionality, and they also open on the Desktop.

To view all of the apps on your laptop, click on the **Start** button and click on the **All apps** button on the Start menu.

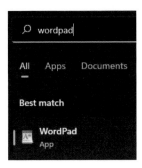

Microsoft Store apps
Microsoft Store apps are accessed and downloaded from the online Microsoft Store. Apps can be browsed and searched for in the Store, and when they are downloaded they are added to the **All apps** alphabetic list on the Start menu.

The Microsoft Store is accessed by clicking on the **Store** tile on the Start menu or on the Taskbar.

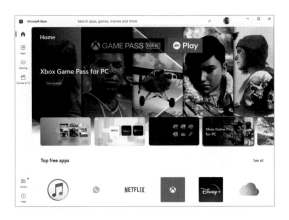

Windows 11 Apps

The Windows 11 apps that are accessed from the **All apps** alphabetic list on the Start menu cover a range of communication, entertainment and information functions. The apps include:

Some of these apps may not be supplied as standard on your Windows 11 system, but you can download them from the Microsoft Store (see pages 84-86).

If you have updated to Windows 11 from a version of Windows 10, some of the apps and their icons may be imported from Windows 10 and may appear slightly different than in Windows 11 installed on a new laptop.

See Chapter 5 for more information about working with the Calendar, Mail, and People apps.

The Microsoft To Do app is a new feature in Windows 11.

 Alarms & Clock. This provides alarms, clocks for times around the world, a timer and a stopwatch.

 Calculator. This is a standard calculator that also has an option for using it as a scientific calculator.

 Calendar. This is a calendar that you can use to add appointments and important dates.

 Camera. This can be used to take photos directly onto your laptop, with a built-in camera.

 Groove Music. This can be used to access the online Music Store where music can be downloaded.

 Mail. This is the online Mail facility. You can use it to connect to a selection of email accounts.

 Maps. This provides online access to maps from around the world. It also shows traffic issues.

 Microsoft Edge. This is the default browser in Windows 11 and is covered in detail in Chapter 5.

 Microsoft News. This is one of the information apps that provide real-time news information.

 Microsoft Store. This provides access to the online Microsoft Store for obtaining more apps and content.

 Microsoft Teams. A collaboration and communication app, including the Chat app, available from the Taskbar only, which is a pop-out version of the Teams audio-, video- and text-chatting functions.

 Microsoft To Do. This is a list-making and reminders app. With a Microsoft Account, the app can also be used with Mail, Outlook and Cortana.

Movies & TV (**Films & TV** in some regions). This is where you will see the movies and TV shows you buy in the Microsoft Store. There is also a link to the Video Store.

 OneDrive. This is an online facility for storing and sharing content from your laptop. This includes photos and documents.

 OneNote. This is a Microsoft note-taking app, part of the Office suite of apps.

 Outlook. Part of Microsoft's 365 subscription service, containing mail, calendar, contacts and tasks options.

 Paint 3D. This is an app that can be used to create, view and share 3D objects.

 Photos. This can be used to view and organize your photos. It can also be used to share and print photos.

 Settings. This can be used to access all of the main settings for customizing and managing Windows 11.

 Snipping Tool. This can be used to capture and annotate screenshots: an image of the screen being viewed.

 Sticky Notes. This is an app for creating short notes that can be "stuck" to the screen so that they are readily visible.

 Voice Recorder. This can be used to record, save and share audio messages.

 Weather. This provides real-time weather forecasts for locations around the world.

 Xbox. This can be used to download and play games, and also play online Xbox games.

A Desktop app for OneDrive can also be downloaded from the Microsoft Store. This can be used to view and manage folders and files in OneDrive. The version described on the pages here is the File Explorer version of OneDrive, where the folders and files are displayed in File Explorer. App versions of OneDrive can also be used to share your content, such as photos and documents, with other people. See pages 110-113 for details.

By default, the Weather app will provide the nearest forecast to your location, if you have given permission for this in **Settings** > **Privacy & security** > **Location**.

Using Windows 11 Apps

In Windows 11, all of the apps have been designed to have as consistent an appearance as possible. However, due to the age of some apps, there are still some differences.

Windows 11 apps

Windows 11 apps open in their own window on the Desktop, and they can be moved and resized in the same way as older-style Windows apps.

In Windows 11 there has been a conscious effort to achieve greater consistency between the newer-style apps and the old, classic-style apps.

1 Click and drag on the top toolbar to move the app's window and reposition it

2 Drag on the bottom or right-hand border to resize the app's window (or the bottom right-hand corner to resize the height and width simultaneously)

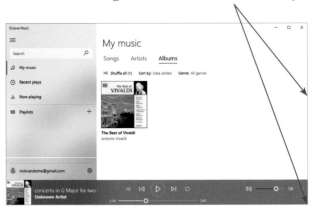

80

...cont'd

Windows 11 app menus
Some Windows 11 apps have their own menus.

1 Click on this button (if available) within the app's window to access its menu

2 Click on the **Menu** button again to minimize the menu to just icons, without text

3 Click this button to move to previously viewed pages within the app

Apps that are installed from a CD or DVD are automatically included on the alphabetical list on the Start menu.

81

Managing an app's window
App control buttons are on the top toolbar.

1 Click on this button to close the app. (The button turns red when you hover your mouse over it)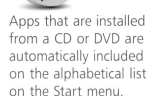

2 Click on this button to maximize the app's window

3 Click on this button to minimize the app's window, onto the Taskbar

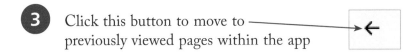

Closing Apps

There are several ways to close a Windows app.

Don't forget

The **Close** button only turns red when you hover your mouse over it.

Beware

It is always worth saving a new document as soon as it is created. It should also be saved at regular intervals as you are working on it.

1 Click on the red **Close** button at the top right of the window

2 Select **File** > **Exit** from the File menu (if available)

3 Press **Alt** + **F4**

4 Right-click on the icon on the Taskbar and select **Close window** (or **Close all windows** if more than one is open)

5 If any changes have been made to the document, you may receive a warning message advising you to save the associated file

Searching for Apps

As you acquire more and more apps, it may become harder to find the ones you want. To help with this, you can use the Search box to search over all of the apps on your laptop. To do this:

1 Click in the Search icon on the Taskbar

2 Enter a word in the Search box

3 As you type, relevant apps are displayed. When the one you are seeking appears, click on it to open the app

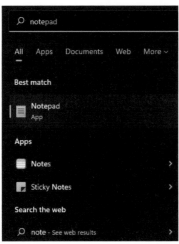

Hot tip

You just have to put in the first couple of letters of an app and the Search function will automatically suggest results based on this. The more that you type, the more specific the results become. Case does not matter when you are typing a search.

4 Click on the **Apps** tab to view results relating only to apps

5 The Apps tab also displays an option for searching for related apps in the Microsoft Store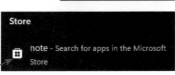

Using the Microsoft Store

The third category of apps that can be used with Windows 11 are those that are downloaded from the Microsoft Store. These cover a wide range of topics, and they provide an excellent way to add functionality to Windows 11. To use the Microsoft Store:

Don't forget

Windows 11 apps can be downloaded from the Microsoft Store.

1 Click on the **Microsoft Store** tile on the Start menu, or the Taskbar

2 The currently featured apps are displayed on the Home screen

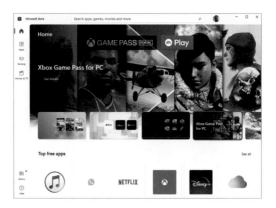

3 Scroll up and down to see additional items and categories

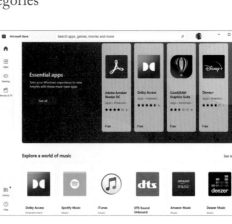

... cont'd

4 Scroll down the Homepage, then click on the **See all** button next to a category; e.g. **Top free apps**

5 The full range of apps for the selected category are displayed. Swipe up and down the page to view them

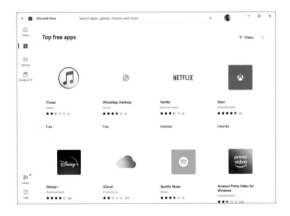

Scroll up and down in Step 6 to view ratings and reviews about the app, and also any additional descriptions.

6 Click on an app to preview it, and for more details

...cont'd

7 On the **See all** page, click on the **Filters** button

8 Click the options for how the app selection is filtered; e.g. **Top free**

9 Click on a new category for filtering the app selection; e.g. **Best-rated**

Don't forget

As more characters are added to the Search box in Step 10, the search results will become more defined; i.e. a closer match to what appears in the Search box.

10 Enter a word or phrase into the **Search apps, games, movies and more** box on the top toolbar to see matching apps. Click on a result to view the related app

Buying Apps

When you find an app that you want to use, you can download it to your laptop. To do this:

1 Click on the app and click on the **Get** (or price) button

2 The app downloads from the Microsoft Store and a **Downloading** message is displayed

3 The app is added to the Start menu and has a **New** tag next to it. This disappears once the app has been opened

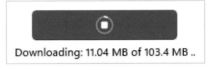

4 Click on the app to open and use it (initially it will be available under the **Recommended** section of the Start menu, as **Recently added**, as well as having its own alpha listing)

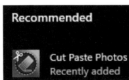

Viewing Your Apps

As you download more and more apps from the Microsoft Store, you may lose track of which ones you have obtained and when. To help with this, you can review all of the apps you have downloaded, from within the Microsoft Store. To do this:

You can reinstall apps from the **Library** section, even if you have previously uninstalled them. If there was a fee for an app, you will not have to pay again to reinstall it.

1 Open the Microsoft Store and click on the **Library** button

2 All of the apps that have been downloaded are displayed

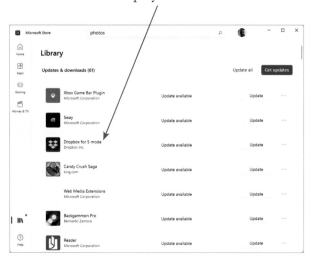

To set apps to be updated automatically, open the Microsoft Store and click on your account icon at the top of the screen. Click on the **App settings** button and drag the **App updates** button **On**.

3 Tap on the **Get updates** button to see if there are any updates for the listed apps

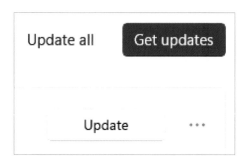

Installing and Uninstalling Apps

Installing apps from a CD or DVD

If the app you want to install is provided on a CD or DVD, you normally just insert the disc. The installation app starts up automatically, and you can follow the instructions to select features and complete the installation. If this does not happen automatically:

1 Insert the disc. If it does not run automatically, right-click on the Start button and click on the **Run** option

2 Navigate to the disc in the File Explorer sidebar and click on the **autorun.exe** file

Installation files can also be named **Set-up.exe** when accessed in Step 2.

3 Click on the **Open** button | Open |

4 The file is added to the **Run** window

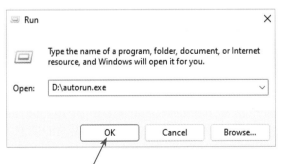

5 Click on the **OK** button to run the file and install the program, which can be accessed from the Start menu

A greater range of apps can be uninstalled in Windows 11. If the **Uninstall** option is not available in Step 1, the app cannot be uninstalled; e.g. the Microsoft Edge app.

...cont'd

Uninstalling apps

In some previous versions of Windows, apps were uninstalled through the Control Panel. However, in Windows 11, some pre-installed Microsoft apps (and Microsoft ones that have been downloaded from the Microsoft Store) can be uninstalled directly from the Start menu. To do this:

1 Right-click on an app to access its menu

2 Click on the **Uninstall** button

3 A window alerts you to the fact that related information will be removed

if the app is uninstalled. Click on the **Uninstall** button if you want to continue

4 If an app has been uninstalled, it will no longer be available from the list of apps on the Start menu. However, it can be downloaded again from the Microsoft Store

If apps have been installed from a CD or DVD, they can also still be uninstalled from within the Control Panel. To do this, select the **Programs** section and click on the **Uninstall a Program** link. The installed apps will be displayed. Select one of the apps and click on the **Uninstall/Change** link.

5 The Online World

This chapter looks at getting online so that you can make the most of the expanding online world. It covers the Microsoft Edge browser, for viewing and managing web pages; the Mail app for email; the online storage and backup facility, OneDrive; and options for creating and viewing online address books and calendars.

92 Introducing the Edge Browser

93 Smart Address Bar

94 Setting a Homepage

95 Using Tabs

96 Managing Tabs

98 Bookmarking Web Pages

99 Viewing Favorites

100 Collections in Edge

102 Shopping Online

104 Booking a Vacation

106 Setting Up Mail

108 Working with Mail

110 Using OneDrive

113 OneDrive Settings

114 Finding People

116 Using the Calendar

The Edge browser has been updated in Windows 11, with a redesigned interface and a number of new features.

For details about connecting to a network and the internet, see pages 152-153.

Click on the **Settings** button in the top right-hand corner of the Microsoft Edge Homepage to access page layout options.

The Start page can be replaced by a specific Homepage – see page 94 for details.

Introducing the Edge Browser

The web browser Internet Explorer (IE) has been synonymous with Microsoft for almost as long as the Windows operating system. Introduced in 1995, shortly after Windows 95, it was the default browser for a generation of web users. However, as with most technologies, the relentless march of time caught up with IE and it has been superseded by a web browser designed specifically for the digital mobile age. It is called Microsoft Edge, and adapts easily to whichever environment it is operating in: desktop, laptop, tablet or phone.

The Microsoft Edge browser has a number of performance and speed enhancements compared with IE, and it also recognizes that modern web users want a lot more from their browser than simply being able to look at web pages.

There is also an option for creating collections, which is a panel where you can store a range of items, including web pages and photos, related to a similar subject.

Click on this icon from the **Taskbar** or the **Start** menu to open the Microsoft Edge browser at the default Start page:

Tab management   Refresh   New tab   Favorites   Collections

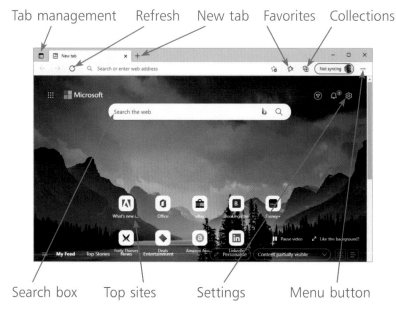

Search box   Top sites   Settings   Menu button

Smart Address Bar

Smart address bars are now a familiar feature in a lot of modern browsers, and Microsoft Edge is no different. This can be used to enter a specific web address to open that page or use it to search for a word or phrase. To use the smart address bar:

1 Click anywhere in the address box at the top of a web page

Hot tip

The personal digital assistant, Cortana, can also be used to open web pages, by asking it to open a specific page. The page will be opened in Microsoft Edge.

2 Start typing a word or website address. As you type, options appear below the address bar. Click on a web page address to open that website

3 Click on one of the options to view the search result for that item

Setting a Homepage

By default, the Edge browser opens at a web page determined by Windows. However, it is possible to set your own Homepage that is available whenever you open the Edge browser. To do this:

1 Click on this button on the top toolbar to access the menu options

2 Click on the **Settings** button

3 Click on the **Start, home, and new tabs** button in the left-hand sidebar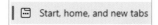

A full list of Edge settings is displayed in the left-hand sidebar.

4 In the **When Microsoft Edge starts** section, check **On** the **Open these pages** option

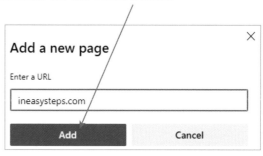

5 Click on the **Add a new page** button

6 Enter the web address (URL) for the required page and click on the **Add** button

Add a new page   ✕

Enter a URL

ineasysteps.com

Add   Cancel

Using Tabs

Being able to open several web pages at the same time in different tabs is a standard feature in most web browsers. To do this with Microsoft Edge:

Hot tip

The Start page for new tabs, as displayed in Step 2, can be changed if required. To do this, open the Microsoft Edge settings and access the **Start, home, and new tabs** section as shown in Step 3 on the previous page. Check **On** the **Open the new tabs page** heading and select a page in the same way as for selecting a Homepage.

1 Click on this button at the top of the Microsoft Edge window

2 Pages can be opened in new tabs using the smart address bar or from news items in **My Feed**, **Top Stories** or other news categories that appear below it

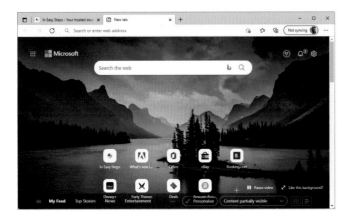

3 All open tabs are displayed at the top of the window. Click and hold on a tab to drag it into a new position

Managing Tabs

Once tabs have been opened in the Edge browser, there are a number of options for viewing and managing them.

The options for managing tabs in the Edge browser have been updated in Windows 11.

1 Click on this button 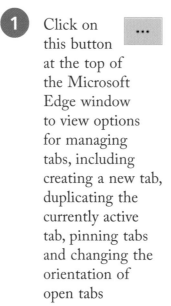 at the top of the Microsoft Edge window to view options for managing tabs, including creating a new tab, duplicating the currently active tab, pinning tabs and changing the orientation of open tabs

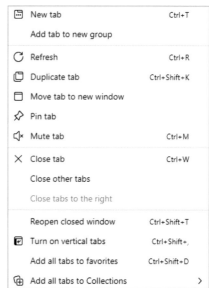

New tab	Ctrl+T
Add tab to new group	
Refresh	Ctrl+R
Duplicate tab	Ctrl+Shift+K
Move tab to new window	
Pin tab	
Mute tab	Ctrl+M
Close tab	Ctrl+W
Close other tabs	
Close tabs to the right	
Reopen closed window	Ctrl+Shift+T
Turn on vertical tabs	Ctrl+Shift+,
Add all tabs to favorites	Ctrl+Shift+D
Add all tabs to Collections	>

2 Click on this button at the left-hand side of the tab bar to access more options

Click on the **Add all tabs to Collections** option in Step 3 to add all of the open tabs to a collection. See pages 100-101 for details about using collections.

3 Click on the **Turn on vertical tabs** option to change the orientation of the tab bar

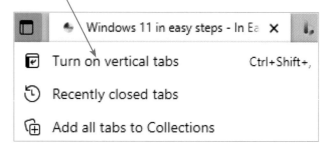

4 The tab bar is displayed down the left-hand side of the Edge browser window

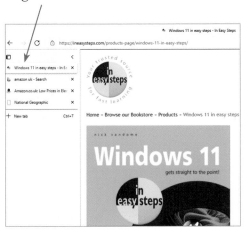

Using vertical tabs is a new feature in Windows 11.

5 Click on this button in Step 4 to minimize the vertical tab bar

Don't forget

6 Click on this button to expand the minimized tab bar

The vertical tabs option can be used even if there is only one open tab.

7 Move the cursor over the minimized tab bar, and click on this button to expand it and keep the maximized option in place

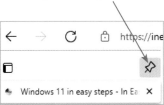

Bookmarking Web Pages

Your favorite web pages can be bookmarked so that you can access them with one click from the **Favorites** button, rather than having to enter the web address each time. To do this:

1 Open the web page that you want to bookmark

2 Click on this button on the toolbar

3 Enter a name for the favorite and where you want it to be saved to

Hot tip

New folders can be created for storing favorites, by clicking in the **Folder** box in Step 3 and clicking on the **New folder** option. The new folder can then be given a new name.

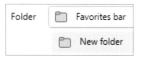

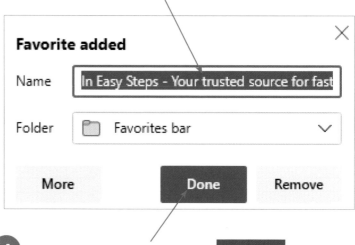

Favorite added

| Name | In Easy Steps - Your trusted source for fast |
| Folder | 📁 Favorites bar ∨ |

More   Done   Remove

4 Click on the **Done** button   Done

5 The star button turns blue, indicating that the web page has been added as a favorite ★

6 Click on this button to access your favorites (see the next page)

Viewing Favorites

Once pages have been bookmarked in the Edge browser, they can be viewed from the **Favorites** button. To do this:

1 Click on this button on the Edge toolbar

2 Click here to view items within the Favorites bar, or other folders that have been created. Click on a bookmarked page to open it

3 Click here to access the Favorites menu

4 Click on the **Show favorites bar** option and select how the Favorites bar is displayed: **Always**, **Never**, or **Only on new tabs**

5 The Favorites bar is displayed below the Address bar

The Favorites bar can also be displayed below the Address bar by opening the Microsoft Edge settings (see page 94) and selecting the **Appearance** option in the left-hand sidebar. In the **Customize toolbar** section, click on the **Show favorites bar** box and select **Always**.

Collections in Edge

Collections within the Edge browser is a feature that can be used to store a range of items, including web pages, notes and images. These can then be accessed within the same panel so that all related items are together. To create collections:

Collections in the Edge browser is a new feature in Windows 11.

1 Right-click on the web page that you are currently viewing and click on the **Add page to Collections** option

2 Click on the **+ Start new collection** button

Collections
+ Start new collection

3 The page is added to a new collection

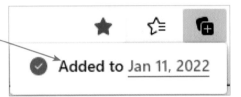

4 To view collections, click on this button on the Edge toolbar

5 The content of the collection is displayed

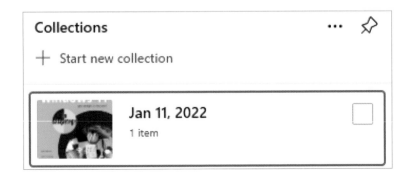

6 Click on the name at the top of the Collections window, and overtype it to give the collection a specific name

7 To add more items to a collection, such as an image, right-click on the item, click on the **Add to Collections** option and select the collection into which it is to be added

8 All of the items within a collection can be viewed in the Collections panel. Click on an item to open it within the Edge browser

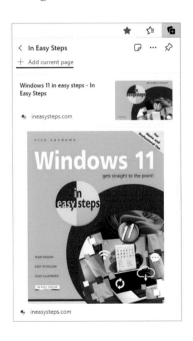

Hot tip

Click on the **Collections** button on the Edge toolbar and click on the **+ Start new collection** option to create another collection.

```
Collections
+ Start new collection
```

Shopping Online

Some people love physically looking around shops, while for others it is a chore. For the latter group, online shopping is one of the great innovations of the web. With a laptop, it is possible to do your shopping in the comfort of your own home, while also avoiding the crowds.

When you are shopping online there are some guidelines that you should follow to try to ensure you are in a safe online environment and do not spend too much money:

A lot of online shopping sites list recommendations for you based on what you have already looked at or bought on the site. This is done by using "cookies", which are small programs that are downloaded from the site and then track the items that you look at on the site (see the next page for further information on cookies).

- Make a note of what you want to buy, and stick to this once you have found it. Online shopping sites are adept at displaying a lot of enticing offers, and it is a lot easier to buy something by clicking a button than it is to physically take it to a checkout.

- Never buy anything that is promoted to you via an email unless it is from a company that you have asked to send you promotional information.

- When paying for items, make sure that the online site has a secure area for accepting payment and credit card details. A lot of sites display information about this within their payment area, and another way to ascertain this is to check in the address bar of the payment page. If it is within a secure area, the address of the page will start with "https" rather than the standard "http".

Using online shopping

The majority of online shopping sites are similar in their operation:

- Goods are identified.

- Goods are placed in a shopping cart/ basket.

Add to Cart

- Once the shopping is completed, you proceed to the checkout.

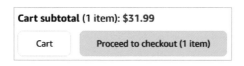

- For some sites you have to register before you can complete your purchase, while with others you do not.

- You enter your shipping details and pay for the goods, usually with a credit or debit card.

In some cases, if you are registered on a site, you can complete your shopping by using a 1-Click system (Buy Now). This means that all of your billing, delivery and payment details are already stored on the site, and you can buy goods simply by clicking one button without having to re-enter your details. One of the most prominent sites to use this method is Amazon.

One-click shopping is an effective way to spend money very quickly. However, you usually have a period of time in which you can cancel your purchases after you have bought them in this way.

Using cookies

A lot of online shopping sites use cookies, which are small programs that store information about your browsing habits on the site. Sites have to tell you if they are using cookies, and they can be a good way to receive targeted information about products in which you are interested. This can be done on the sites when you are logged in, or via email.

For more help with staying safe online, check out **100 Top Tips – Stay Safe Online and Protect Your Privacy** at www.ineasysteps.com

103

Booking a Vacation

Just as many retailers have created an online presence, the same is also true for vacation companies and travel agents. It is now possible to book almost any type of vacation on the web, from cruises to city breaks.

Several sites offer full travel services where they can deal with flights, hotels, insurance, car hire and excursions. These sites include:

- **www.expedia.com**

- **www.kayak.com**

- **www.orbitz.com**

- **www.travelocity.com**

These sites usually list special offers and last-minute deals on their Homepages, or if you sign up to an email newsletter. There is also a facility for specifying your precise requirements. To do this:

Hot tip

It is always worth searching different sites to get the best possible prices. In some cases, it is cheapest to buy different elements of a vacation from different sites; e.g. flights from one and accommodation from another.

1 Select your vacation requirements. This can include flight or hotel only, or a combination of both, with or without car hire options

2 Enter flight details

3 Enter dates for your vacation

4 Click on the **Search** button

TripAdvisor

One of the best resources for travelers is TripAdvisor. Not only does the site provide a full range of opportunities for booking flights and hotels, it also has an extensive network of reviews from people who have visited the countries, hotels and

restaurants on the site. These are independent, and usually very fair and honest. In a lot of cases, if there are issues with a hotel or restaurant, the proprietor posts a reply to explain what is being done to address any problems.

Cruises

There are also websites dedicated specifically to cruises:

- **www.carnival.com**

- **www.cruises.com**

- **www.princess.com**

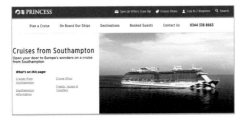

Hotels

There are a range of websites that specialize in hotel bookings, a lot of them at short notice to get the best price:

- **www.choicehotels.com**

- **www.hotels.com**

- **www.laterooms.com**

- **www.trivago.com**

Vacation and hotel websites usually have versions that are specific to your geographical location.

The web is also excellent for researching family history and genealogy. Some sites to try are Ancestry; Genealogy; FamilySearch; and RootsWeb.

Setting Up Mail

Email has become an essential part of everyday life, both socially and in the business world. Windows 11 accommodates this with the Mail app. This can be used to link to online services such as Gmail and Outlook (the renamed version of Hotmail), and also other email accounts. To set up an email account with Mail:

1 Click on the **Mail** app on the Start menu

2 Click on the **Accounts** button

The **Other account** option in Step 4 can be used to add a non-webmail account. This is usually a POP3 or an IMAP account, and you will need your email address, username, password, and usually the incoming and outgoing email servers. If you do not know these, they should be supplied by your email provider. They should also be available in the account settings of the email account you want to add to the Mail app.

3 Click on the **+ Add account** button

4 Select the type of account to which you want to link via the Mail app. This can be an online email account that you have already set up

5 Enter your current sign-in details for the selected email account and click on the **Sign in** button

You can add more than one account to the Mail app. If you do this, you will be able to select different accounts to view within Mail.

6 Once it has been connected, details of the account are shown under the **Mail** button, including the mailboxes within the account. Click on the **Accounts** button to view all linked accounts

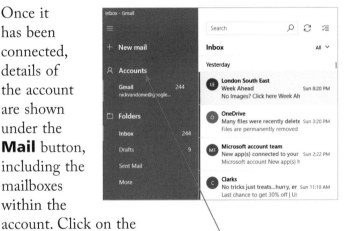

7 A list of emails appears in the middle panel. Double-click on an email to view it at full size

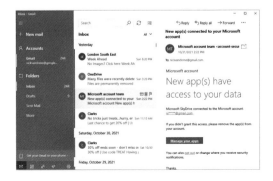

Click on this button at the top of the left-hand panel to expand and collapse menu items, with their text descriptions:

Working with Mail

Once you have set up an account in the Mail app, you can then start creating and managing your emails with it.

Contacts that are added automatically as email recipients are taken from the People app, provided there is an email address connected to their entry.

1 On the main mail page, open an email and click on the **Reply**, **Reply all** or **Forward** buttons to respond

2 Open an email and click on the **Delete** button to remove it

Composing an email

To compose and send an email message:

The email address can either be in the format of *myname@email. com* or you can enter the name of one of your contacts from the People app (see pages 114-115), and the email address will be entered automatically.

1 Click on this button to create a new message

2 Click in the **To:** field and enter an email address

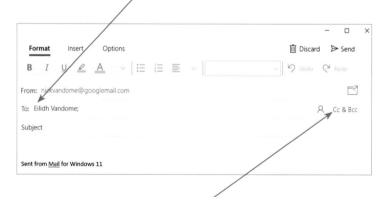

3 Click on the **Cc & Bcc** link to access options for copying and blind copying

4 Enter a subject heading and body text to the email

To: Eilidh Vandome;

Sunset

Have a look at this!

Sent from Mail for Windows 11

5 Click on the **Insert** button on the top toolbar in the new email window and select one of the options, such as **Pictures**

Format **Insert** Options

📎 Files   ▦ Table   🖼 Pictures   ⬥ Link

6 Click on a folder from which you want to attach a file, and click on the **Insert** button

046.JPG   047.JPG   048.JPG

All files (*.jpg;*.jpeg;*.jfif;*.jpe;* ⌄

➤ Insert   Cancel

Insert

7 The file is shown in the body of the email

8 Select an item of text and select the text-formatting options from the top toolbar

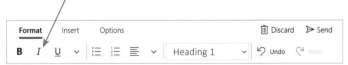

Format   Insert   Options   🗑 Discard   ➤ Send

B *I* U̲ ⌄   ☰ ☰ ☰ ⌄   Heading 1   ⌄   ↩ Undo   ↪ Redo

9 Click on this button to send the email

➤ Send

Hot tip

When composing an email, or at any other time, press the **Windows key** (**WinKey**) and the period/full stop key on the keyboard to access a panel for adding emojis (graphical symbols) to an item. This can also be used with other messaging apps.

OneDrive has a **Personal Vault** folder that has added levels of security for storing your most sensitive and important documents and photos. It requires an extra level of security to access the Personal Vault; e.g. a PIN code or a code that is sent to you via email or text message. The Personal Vault can be accessed from any of the OneDrive interfaces.

Click on these buttons on the right-hand side of the OneDrive toolbar in Step 2 (i.e. when you are signed in to the web version of OneDrive) to, from left to right: sort content; display it as a grid; or view its details:

Using OneDrive

Cloud computing is now a mainstream part of our online experience. This involves saving content to an online server connected to the service that you are using – i.e. through your Microsoft Account. You can then access this content from any computer or mobile device using your account login details, and also share it with other people by giving them access to your cloud service. It can also be used to back up your files, in case they get corrupted or damaged on your laptop.

The cloud service with Windows 11 is known as OneDrive, and you can use it with a Microsoft Account. It consists of the OneDrive folder in File Explorer, the OneDrive app, and the online OneDrive website. Content added to any of the elements will be available in the others. To use them:

1 Click on the **OneDrive** folder in File Explorer to view its contents. Or, click on this button on the Start menu

2 Download the OneDrive app from the Microsoft Store and click on this icon on the Start menu to open it. It should display the same items as in the OneDrive folder in File Explorer

3. To view the contents of OneDrive online, go to the website at **onedrive.live.com** and sign in with your Microsoft Account details. Your OneDrive

content is the same as in your OneDrive folder on your laptop

Files and folders can be added to OneDrive from any of the three elements.

Adding items to OneDrive in File Explorer

1. In File Explorer, the OneDrive folder is located below Quick access (and any other folders that have been added)

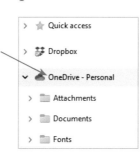

2. Click on the OneDrive folder to view its contents

3. Add files to the OneDrive folder by dragging and dropping them from another folder, or by using Copy and Paste

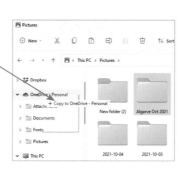

Hot tip

Your OneDrive folder can be pinned to the Quick access section in File Explorer. To do this, right-click on the OneDrive icon in File Explorer and click on **Pin to Quick access**.

Hot tip

By default, you get 5GB of free OneDrive storage space with Windows 11. This is an excellent way to back up your important documents, since they are stored away from your laptop. For up-to-date information on plan allowances and pricing, visit **https://onedrive.live.com/about/plans/**

...cont'd

Adding items to the OneDrive app

1 Open the OneDrive app and click on the **Upload** button

2 Select whether to upload **Files** or a **Folder** from your laptop

3 Navigate to the required item in File Explorer, select it, and click on the **Select Folder** button to add it to your OneDrive folder

Adding items to OneDrive online

1 Access your online OneDrive account and click on the **Upload** button

2 Select whether to upload **Files** or a **Folder** and navigate to the required items as above

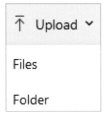

OneDrive Settings

A range of settings can be applied to OneDrive, including adding and syncing folders. To do this:

1 Right-click on the OneDrive icon on the Notifications area of the Taskbar and click on **Settings**

2 Click on the **Settings** tab for options for starting OneDrive when you sign in, and for receiving notifications if other people share items to your OneDrive account

3 Click on the **Account** tab and click on the **Choose folders** button to select a folder from your laptop that you want to sync with your OneDrive account

4 Click on the **OK** button to apply any changes to the OneDrive settings

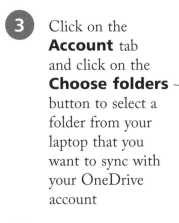

Don't forget

If the OneDrive icon is not visible on the Taskbar, access it in the **All apps** section of the Start menu, right-click on it and click on **Pin to taskbar**.

Don't forget

The Account section can also be used to unlink your laptop so that files on your laptop are not synced with the online OneDrive. Click on the **Unlink this PC** option to do this.

Finding People

An electronic address book is always a good feature to have on a laptop, and with Windows 11 this function is provided by the People app. This not only allows you to add your own contacts manually; you can also link to any of your online accounts, such as Gmail or iCloud, and import the contacts that you have there. In Windows 11, the People app is accessed from the Mail app.

Don't forget

If the People app is being used for the first time, there will be a page with an option to add contacts from an existing account, such as Google or iCloud. If an account has already been added for the Mail app then this can be used, and there is also an **Import contacts** option for importing from another account.

Hot tip

You can also select accounts to add to the People app from the Homepage when you first open it.

Hot tip

To delete a contact, right-click on their name in the Contacts list and click on the **Delete** button to remove them.

1 Open the Mail app and click on this button in the bottom left-hand corner

2 The current contacts are displayed. Double-click on a contact to view their details

3 Click on a letter at the top of a section to access the alpha search list. Click on a letter to view contacts starting with the selected letter

4 Click on the **Settings** button to add new accounts from which you want to import contacts, such as a Gmail or an iCloud account (in the same way as setting up a new email account). Click on the **+ Add an account** button to add the required account. The contacts from the linked account are imported to the People app

...cont'd

Adding contacts manually

As well as importing contacts, it is also possible to enter them manually into the People app.

1 Click on the **New contact** button on the top toolbar

2 Enter details for the new contact, including name, email address and phone number

3 Click on the Down arrow next to a field to access additional options for that item

4 Click on the **Save** button at the bottom of the window to create a new contact

Hot tip

Once a contact has been added, select it as in Step 2 on the previous page and click on this button to edit the contact's details:

Hot tip

When a contact has been selected, click on the pin icon on the top toolbar and select either **Pin to Taskbar** or **Pin to Start** to pin the contact here. More than three contacts can now be pinned in this way.

115

Using the Calendar

The Calendar app can be used to record important events and reminders. To view the calendar:

Accounts can be added to the Calendar app in the same way as for the Mail and People apps.

1 Click on the **Calendar** app on the Start menu

2 Click here to view the calendar in **Day**, **Week**, or **Month** mode

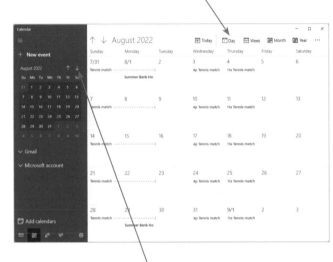

Click on the **Week** option in Step 2 to access options for displaying the calendar as a **Work week** – i.e. five days (Monday to Friday) – or a full **Week**.

3 Click on these buttons to move between months (or swipe left or right on a touchpad)

Adding events

Events can be added to the calendar and various settings can be applied to them, such as recurrence and reminders.

1. Click on a date to create a new event and click on the **+ New event** button

2. Enter an **Event name** and a **Location** at the top of the window

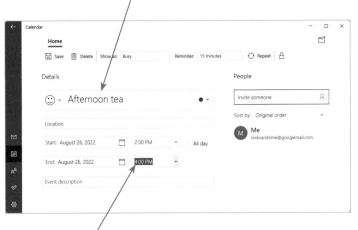

3. Click here and select a time for the start and end of the event

4. If **All day** is selected, the time fields will not be available

Reminders can be set for calendar events, and these appear in the **Notifications** area. Click on this box in Step 2 to set a time period for a reminder:

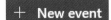

117

...cont'd

5 For a recurring event, click on the **Repeat** button at the top of the window

6 Select an option for the recurrence, such as **Weekly**

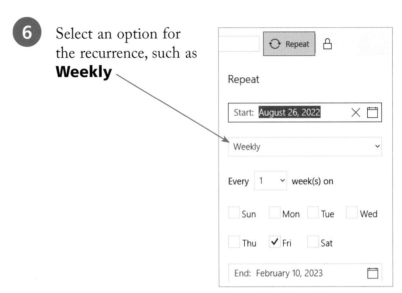

When an event is due, an alert will appear on the screen.

7 Click on the **Save** button to save an event to the calendar, or click on the **Delete** button to remove it

8 To delete an existing event or series of events (i.e. one that has repeat occurrences), right-click on it and click on the **Delete** button

6 A Digital Lifestyle

This chapter shows how to work with a range of entertainment apps so that you can fully embrace the digital world.

120 Viewing Photos

122 Editing Photos

124 Groove Music

125 Playing Music

126 Viewing Movies and TV

128 Gaming with Windows 11

Viewing Photos

The Photos app can be used to manage and edit your photos, including those stored in your **Pictures** Library. To do this:

Hot tip

To import photos into the Photos app, click on this button on the top toolbar and select a location from where you want to import the photos. This can be a folder on your own laptop; a camera or flashdrive attached with a USB cable; or a memory card from a camera.

1 Click on the **Photos** app on the Start menu or the Taskbar

2 The main categories are at the left-hand side of the screen, on the top toolbar

3 Other options are at the right-hand side of the toolbar

Searching for items   Selecting item(s)   Importing photos

Hot tip

Click on the **People** button in Step 2 to use facial technology to identify people in your photos. Click on the **Video Editor** button to access options for creating video projects.

4 Click on the **Collection** button to view all of the photos in the Photos app, arranged by date. Scroll up and down to view the photos

Don't forget

Click on the **Folders** button in Step 2 to view photos that have been copied into this folder from another location.

5 Click on the **Albums** button to view photos from specific albums

6 Within the Albums section, double-click on an album to view its contents. The first photo is also displayed as a banner at the top of the album

7 Double-click on a photo within an album or collection to view it at full size, with the toolbar shown at the top of the window

Albums can include photos and videos.

Photos within either a collection or an album in the Photos app can be selected and then shared with other people in various ways, or deleted. To do this: in a collection or an open album, click on the **Select** button on the top toolbar. Click in the box in the top-right corner to select a photo or photos. Click on the **Share** button to share the selected photo(s).

Editing Photos

In Windows 11, the Photos app has a range of editing functions so that you can improve and enhance your photos. To use these:

1 Open a photo at full size, with the top toolbar displayed

2 Click on the **Edit image** button on the top toolbar. Click on these buttons to view the editing options

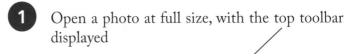
Edit image (Ctrl+E)

3 By default, the **Crop & rotate** option is opened in Step 2 on the previous page. This can be used to crop the current photo or rotate it in a variety of ways, such as straightening, or flipping horizontally or vertically

4 Click on the **Filters** button from the editing options to apply filter effects. Click on an effect to apply it to the photo

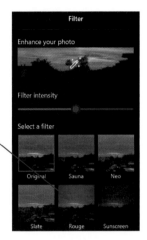

5 Click on the **Adjustments** button from the editing options to apply a range of color adjustments. Click next to an adjustment category to view more options. Drag the sliders to apply the amount of the editing option, as required

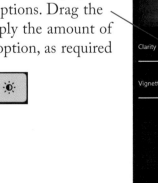

Hot tip

Most photos benefit from some degree of cropping, so that the main subject is given greater prominence by removing unwanted items in the background.

Don't forget

Click on the **Save a copy** button at the bottom of the editing panel to save a copy of an edited image, without changing the original. Click on the down-pointing arrow to access an option to **Save** the edited image, which now becomes the original.

Groove Music

The Groove Music app is used to access music that you have added to your laptop. To use it:

1 Click on the Groove Music app on the Start menu

2 Click on the **Menu** button to expand the menu so that the titles are visible, not just the icons

124

3 Click on a category to view those items; e.g. **My music** for the music that you have available on your laptop

4 Items within the selected category are displayed. Use the tabs on the top toolbar to view items according to these categories

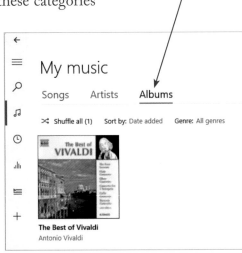

Playing Music

Music that has been added to your laptop can be played through the Groove Music app, and you can automatically specify new music to be included when it is added. To do this:

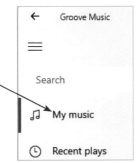

1 Open the Groove Music app and click on the **My music** button

2 Click on the **Songs**, **Artists** or **Albums** tabs as shown in Step 4 on the previous page, to view items within each category

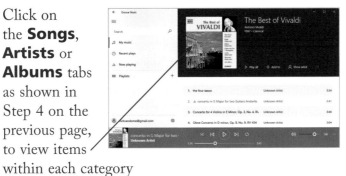

3 Click on an item to access it

4 Click on a track or album to start playing it

5 Use these buttons below to, from left to right: shuffle the available tracks; go to the start of a track; pause/play a track; go to the end of a track; repeat a track; or change or mute the volume

Hot tip

When a folder is added to the Music Library, any music that is copied there will be displayed by the Groove Music app.

125

Hot tip

The Spotify app can be used to stream music using Windows 11. This can be downloaded from the Microsoft Store.

Viewing Movies and TV

For movie and TV lovers, the Movies & TV app can be used to download and watch your favorite movies and shows. It connects to the Microsoft Store from where you can preview and buy a large range of content.

The Movies & TV app is called **Films & TV** in some regions.

Click on the **Purchased** button in Step 2 to view all of the items you have bought.

1 Click on the **Movies & TV** app on the Start menu

2 The Microsoft Store opens at the **Explore** section for viewing available items

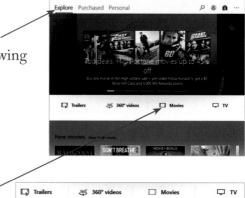

3 Click on the **Movies** (or **TV**) button to view available items

4 Click on an item to see more information, view a preview clip, or buy or rent a movie

Movies and TV shows can be streamed (viewed from the computer server where the item is stored, rather than downloading it) if you have a fast internet connection. They can also be downloaded to a single device so that they can be viewed while you are offline.

5 Click on the **Trailers** button in Step 3 on the previous page to view previews of movies

6 Click on an item to view its trailer

Reminiscence

7 The trailer plays in the Movies & TV window

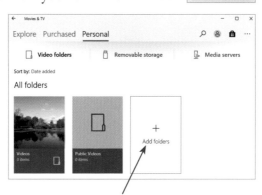

Don't forget

The interface for viewing a trailer is the same as for viewing a movie or TV show that has been bought or rented. Click on the main window to access the control buttons at the bottom of the screen.

127

8 Click on the **Personal** button on the top toolbar to view your own videos that have been added to your laptop. Items from the **Video folders** are displayed, and new folders can be added, using the **+ Add folders** button

Personal

Gaming with Windows 11

In Windows 11, the Xbox app can be used for playing games and interacting online with other gamers. To play games in Windows 11:

1 Click on the **Start** button and click on the **Xbox Console Companion** app

2 Click on the **Home** button to view the Xbox Homepage. This contains the **Toolbar** (down the left-hand side), the **Activity feed** (in the middle panel), and options for joining clubs and connecting with other gamers (in the right-hand panel)

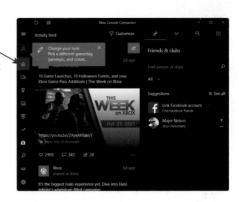

3 Click on the **My games** button to view system games or those that you have downloaded from the Microsoft Store

4 Click on the **Achievements** button to view your scores from games you have played, and compare them with other gamers

5 Click on the **Clubs** button to view details of online game-playing clubs. This is where you can join up with other players to compare scores and also play online games against other players (multiplayer games)

Don't forget

You have to be signed in with your Microsoft Account in order to use the Xbox app and all of its features.

7 On Vacation

Due to their portability, laptops are ideal for taking on vacation. This chapter looks at the issues of taking your laptop with you and keeping it safe.

130 Transporting Your Laptop

131 Keeping Your Laptop Safe

132 Temperature Extremes

133 Laptops at Sea

134 Power Sockets

135 Airport Security

136 Keeping in Touch with Chat

Transporting Your Laptop

When you are going on vacation, your laptop can be a valuable companion. It can be used to download vacation photographs and home movies from a digital camera or a smartphone, keep a diary of your vacation, and keep a record of your itinerary and important documents. In many parts of the world, it can access the internet via wireless hotspots so that you can view the web and send emails. However, when you are traveling with your laptop it is sensible to transport this valuable asset as safely and securely as possible. Some options include:

Laptop case

A standard laptop case is a good option for when you are on vacation; it is compact, lightweight and designed to accommodate your laptop and its accessories.

Metal case

If you are concerned that your laptop may be in danger of physical damage on your vacation, you may want to consider a more robust metal case. These are similar to those used by photographers and, depending on the size and design, you may also be able to include your photographic equipment.

Backpack

A serious option for transporting your laptop on vacation is a small backpack. This can either be a standard backpack or a backpack specifically designed for a laptop. The latter is clearly a better option as the laptop will fit more securely, and there are also pockets designed for accessories.

Don't forget

A backpack for carrying a laptop can be more comfortable than a shoulder bag as it distributes the weight more evenly.

Keeping Your Laptop Safe

By most measures, laptops are valuable items. However, in a lot of countries around the world their relative value can be a lot more than it is to their owners: in some countries the value of a laptop could easily equate to a month's, or even a year's, wages. Even in countries where their relative value is not so high, they can still be seen as a lucrative opportunity for thieves. Therefore, it is important to try to keep your laptop as safe as possible when you are on vacation. Some points to consider in relation to this are:

- If possible, try to keep your laptop with you at all times; i.e. transport it in a piece of luggage that you can carry rather than having to put it into a large case.

- Never hand over your laptop, or any other items of your belongings, to any local who promises to look after them.

- If you do have to detach yourself from your laptop, try to put it somewhere secure, such as a hotel safe.

- When you are traveling, try to keep your laptop as unobtrusive as possible. This is where a backpack carrying case can prove useful, as it is not immediately apparent that you are carrying a laptop.

- Do not use your laptop in areas where you think it may attract undue interest from the locals, particularly in obviously poor areas. For instance, if you are in a local café, the appearance of a laptop may create unwanted attention for you. If in doubt, wait until you get back to your hotel.

- If you are accosted by criminals who demand your laptop, then hand it over. No piece of equipment is worth suffering physical injury for.

- Make sure your laptop is covered by your vacation insurance. If not, get separate insurance for it.

- Trust your instincts with your laptop. If something doesn't feel right, then don't do it.

Hot tip

Save your important documents, such as vacation photos, onto a flashdrive on a daily basis when on vacation, and keep this away from your laptop. This way, you will still have these items if your laptop is lost or stolen.

Temperature Extremes

Traveling includes seeing different places and cultures, but it also invariably involves different extremes of temperature: a visit to the pyramids of Egypt can see the mercury in the upper reaches of the thermometer, while a cruise to Alaska would present much colder conditions. Whether it is hot or cold, looking after your laptop is an important consideration in extremes of temperature.

Beware

If a laptop gets too hot it could buckle the plastic casing, making it difficult to close.

Heat

When traveling in hot countries, the best way of avoiding damage to your laptop is to prevent it from getting too hot in the first place:

- Do not place your laptop in direct sunlight.

- Keep your laptop insulated from the heat.

- Do not leave your laptop in an enclosed space, such as a car. Not only can this get very hot, but the sun's power can be increased by the vehicle's glass.

Hot tip

Try wrapping your laptop in something white, such as a T-shirt or a towel, to insulate it against the heat.

Cold

Again, it is best to try to avoid your laptop getting too cold in the first place, and this can be done by following similar precautions as for heat. However, if your laptop does suffer from extremes of cold, allow it to warm up to normal room temperature again before you try to use it. This may take a couple of hours but it will be worth the wait, rather than risking damaging the delicate computing elements inside.

Laptops at Sea

Water is the greatest enemy of any electrical device, and laptops are no different. This is of particular relevance to anyone who is taking their laptop on vacation near water, such as on a cruise. This not only has the obvious element of water in the sea, but also the proliferation of swimming pools that are a feature of cruise ships. If you are going on vacation near water, then bear in mind the following:

- **Avoid water**. The best way to keep your laptop dry is to keep it away from water whenever possible. For instance, if you want to update your diary or download some photographs, then it would be best to do this in an indoor environment, rather than when sitting around the pool.

- **Keeping dry**. If you think you will be transporting your laptop near water, then it is a good precaution to protect it with some form of waterproof bag. There is a range of "dry-bags" that are excellent for this type of occasion, as they remain waterproof even if fully immersed in water. These can be bought from a number of outdoor suppliers.

- **Drying out**. If the worst does occur and your laptop does get a good soaking, then all is not lost. However, you will have to ensure that it is fully dried out before you try to use it again.

Power Sockets

Different countries and regions around the world use different types of power sockets, and this is an issue when you are on vacation with your laptop. Wherever you are going in the world, it is vital to have an adapter that will fit the sockets in the countries you intend to visit, otherwise you will not be able to charge your laptop.

There are over a dozen different types of plugs and sockets used around the world, with the four most popular being:

North America, Japan
This is a two-point plug and socket. The pins on the plug are flat and parallel.

Continental Europe
This is a two-point plug and socket. The pins are rounded.

Australasia, China, Argentina
This is a three-point socket that can accommodate either a two- or a three-pin plug. In a two-pin plug, the pins are angled in a V shape.

UK
This is a three-point plug. The pins are rectangular.

Power adapters can be bought for all regions around the world. There are also kits that provide all of the adapters together. These provide connections for anywhere, worldwide.

If you are going on a cruise, check before you travel which type of power socket your ship has, and get the right adapter.

Airport Security

Because of the increased global security following terrorist attacks, levels of airport security have been greatly increased around the world. This has implications for all travelers, and if you are traveling with a laptop this will add to the security scrutiny you will face. When dealing with airport security when traveling with a laptop, there are some issues that you should always keep in mind:

- Keep your laptop with you at all times. Unguarded baggage at airports immediately raises suspicion and it can make life very easy for thieves.

- Carry your laptop in a small bag so that you can take it on board as hand luggage. On no account should it be put in with your luggage that goes in the hold.

- X-ray machines at airports will not harm your laptop. However, if anyone tries to scan it with a metal detector, ask them if they can inspect it by hand instead.

- Keep a careful eye on your laptop when it goes through the X-ray conveyor belt, and try to be there at the other side as soon as it emerges. There have been some stories of people causing a commotion at the security gate just after someone has placed their laptop on the conveyor belt. While everyone's attention (including yours) is distracted, an accomplice takes the laptop from the conveyor belt. If you are worried about this, you can ask for the security guard to hand-check your laptop rather than putting it on the conveyor belt.

- Make sure the battery of your laptop is fully charged. This is because you may be asked to turn on your laptop to verify that it is just that, and not some other device disguised as a laptop.

- When you are on the plane, keep the laptop in the storage area under your seat rather than in the overhead locker, so that you know where it is at all times.

Beware

If there is any kind of distraction when you are going through security checks at an airport, it could be because someone is trying to divert your attention in order to steal your laptop.

Hot tip

When traveling through airport security, leave your laptop in **Sleep** mode so that it can be powered up quickly if anyone needs to check that it works properly.

Keeping in Touch with Chat

Windows 11 is integrated closely with the collaboration and communication app Microsoft Teams. Part of this is the Chat app, which is a new feature in Windows 11 and provides text-, audio- and video-chat functions, linked to Microsoft Teams but provided through an independent app. To get started with Chat:

The Chat app is a new feature in Windows 11.

Hot tip

If the Microsoft Teams app has already been accessed, some of the initial steps for setting up the Chat app may not be required.

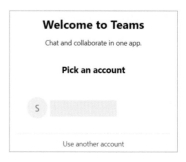

Hot tip

For a detailed look at Microsoft Teams, see **Microsoft Teams in easy steps** at www. ineasysteps.com

1 Click on the **Chat** icon on the Taskbar

2 Click on the **Get started** button

3 Select the Microsoft Account to use with the Chat app (which links to the parent app, Microsoft Teams). The Microsoft Account is usually the one you use for signing in with Windows 11

4 Enter the name you want to appear in the Chat app and click on the **Next** button

5 Click on the **Let's go** button

6 Click on the **Sync contacts** button to synchronize your contacts from other apps and locations

The Microsoft Teams app has replaced Skype as the default collaboration and communication app within Windows.

7 Click on the options for synchronizing contacts. These will then be available in the Chat app

8 Click on the **Chat** app again to access it, ready for text, audio or video chats. Enter a name in the **To:** box to select someone for a conversation

...cont'd

9 Click in the text box to enter text for the message

The **Format** icon in Step 9 includes options for adding bold, italics, underlining, font color and font size. Formatting selections can be made before text is added, or to selected text.

10 Use the icons below the text box to add a range of content to the message

11 Click on the **Attach Files** button in Step 9 above and click on the **Upload from my computer** option to select files from your own laptop

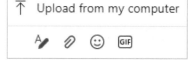

12 Click on the **Emoji** button in Step 9 above and click on an emoji to add it to the text message

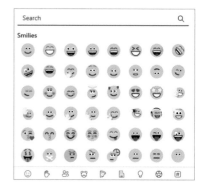

13 Scroll down the emoji page, or click on the toolbar at the bottom of the panel, to access different categories of emojis

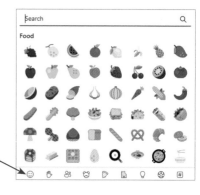

8 Sharing with Your Family

This chapter deals with

sharing your laptop.

140 About Multiple Users

142 Adding Users

144 Family Safety

About Multiple Users

Because of the power and flexibility that is available in a laptop computer, it seems a waste to restrict it to a single user. Thankfully, it is possible for multiple users to use the same laptop. One way to do this is simply to let different people use the laptop whenever they have access to it. However, since everyone creates their own files and documents, and different people use different types of apps, it makes much more sense to allow people to set up their own user accounts. This creates their own personal computing area that is protected from anyone else accessing it. User accounts create a sense of personalization, and also security, as each account can be protected by a password.

Without user accounts, the laptop will display the default account automatically. However, if different user accounts have been set up on the laptop, a list of these accounts will be displayed by clicking on your own account icon on the Start menu.

Don't forget

If no other user accounts have been set up, yours will be the only one, and you will be the administrator. This means that you can set up new accounts and alter a variety of settings on the laptop.

The relevant user can then click on their own account to access it. At this point they will have to enter the correct password to gain access to their account. A user can have a Local Account or a Microsoft Account. If it is the latter, the user will have access to a selection of Microsoft services, through the Windows 11 apps. A password can be specified for either a Local Account or a Microsoft one. To see how to add new user accounts, see pages 142-143.

Customization

Once individual user accounts have been set up, it is possible for each user to customize their account; i.e. to set the way in which their account appears and operates. This means that each user can set their own preferences, such as for the way the Start menu and Desktop background appear, and also items on the Taskbar:

This shows two different user accounts and the changes in the Start menu, background and Taskbar apps.

The whole Desktop environment can be customized. This is done within the **Personalization** section of the **Settings** app.

Adding Users

If more than one person uses the laptop, each person can have a user account defined with a username and a password. To create a new user account, as either a Microsoft Account or a Local Account:

Beware

An email address is a required field when creating a new user with a Microsoft Account.

Don't forget

At Step 3 (further down the screen) there is also an option to **Add other user**, not just a family member.

1 Access the **Settings** app and select **Accounts**

2 Click on the **Family & other users** button

Family & other users
Device access, work or school users, kiosk assigned access

3 Click on the **Add account** button

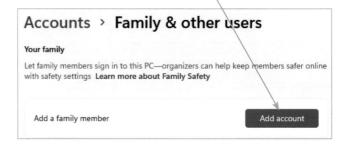

Accounts › **Family & other users**

Your family

Let family members sign in to this PC—organizers can help keep members safer online with safety settings **Learn more about Family Safety**

Add a family member   Add account

4 Enter the email address for the new user and click on the **Next** button

Microsoft account   ×

Add someone

Enter their email address

No Microsoft account? Create one for a child

Cancel   Next

5 Enter the name of the new user, an email address and a password to create a Microsoft Account for the user

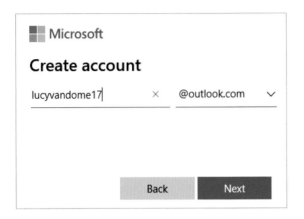

6 Click on the **Next** button to complete the setup wizard

7 The user is added to the Accounts page

8 Click on a user to change the type of their account (e.g. from a Local Account to a Microsoft Account) or to delete their account

Multiple people can have separate accounts on the same laptop, each with their own settings.

Family Safety

Once multiple user accounts have been set up, it is possible to apply separate online security settings to different accounts. This can be useful if you are going to be setting up an account for grandchildren and you want to have a certain amount of control over how they use the laptop. To do this:

1 Access the **Accounts** > **Family & other users** section of the **Settings** app

2 Click on the **Manage family settings online or remove an account** link

3 On the **Family Safety** page, click on the account to which you want to apply Family Safety changes

The default browser for viewing the family settings online is Microsoft Edge.

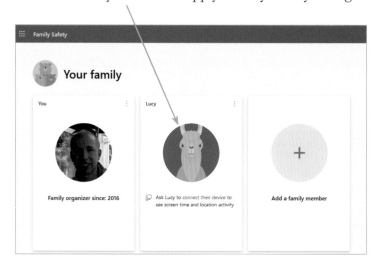

Recent activity controls

One of the options within the Family Safety controls is to view recent activity by a user. To view this:

1 For the person selected in Step 3 on the previous page, menu options are displayed in the left-hand panel

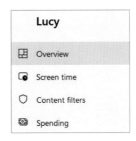

2 Click on the **Overview** option and scroll down the page to the **Activity settings** section. Drag the **Activity reporting** button **On**

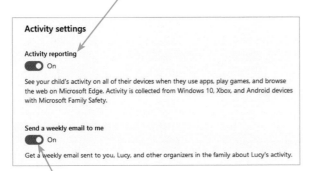

3 Check **On** the **Send a weekly email to me** button to receive a weekly report about the user's computer usage

4 Scroll down the page to access **Help** options for using the Family Safety features

If you are setting Family Safety for young people, such as grandchildren, make sure you tell them what you have done so that they understand the reasons behind your actions.

Some of the notation in the **Family Safety** section still uses Windows 10.

…cont'd

Web-browsing controls

The websites accessed by a specific user can also be
controlled through Family Safety. To do this:

1 On the
Overview
page, click on
the **Content filters** option and click
on the **Web and search** tab

2 Drag the **Filter inappropriate websites and
searches** button **On**

3 Enter the web addresses of any websites you want to
include, and click on the **+** button

4 Repeat the process in Step 3 here, for any websites
that you want to be blocked

Apps and games controls

Computer games and apps are another very popular pastime for young people. However, just as with movies, some games and apps are unsuitable for younger children and should have ratings to specify the age groups for which they are suitable. It is then possible to control which games are played. To do this:

1 In the **Content filters** section, click on the **Apps and games** tab

2 Click in the **Apps and games rated up to age** box to select a appropriate age, as required

3 Click on one of the **Content ratings** options to limit games and apps accordingly, based on their content

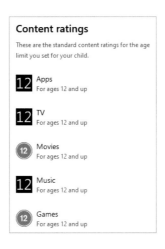

The age ratings in Step 3 will be applicable to your geographical location.

...cont'd

Screen time controls

A familiar worry when young people are using computers is the amount of time that they are spending on them. However, this can also be controlled in the Screen time controls for a selected user. To do this:

1 On the **Overview** page, click on the **Screen time** option

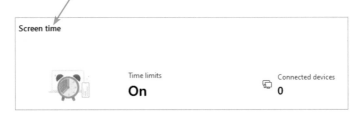

If time controls have been set, the affected user will not be able to access their account outside the times that have been specified.

2 Drag the **Use one schedule on all devices** button **On** to apply the screen time schedule to all devices connected to the user's Microsoft Account

3 Click here to select time limits for specific days, for when devices can be used

9 Networking and Wireless

This chapter shows how to use the Windows 11 networking functions, enabling you to connect to networks and use Nearby Sharing.

150 Network Components

151 Going Wireless

152 Connecting to a Network

154 Viewing Network Status

155 Sharing Settings

156 Nearby Sharing

158 Network Troubleshooting

The network adapter can be connected to the USB port, inserted in the PC Card slot, or installed inside your laptop.

Ethernet adapters connect to a network hub, switch or wired router. Wireless adapters connect through a wireless router or a combination of router/switch.

You may already have some of these elements in operation, if you have an existing network running a previous version of Windows.

Network Components

There are numerous possibilities for setting up a home network. To start with, there are two major network technologies:

- **Wired** – e.g. Ethernet, using twisted-pair cables to send data at rates of 10, 100 or 1,000 Mbps (megabits per second).

- **Wireless** – Using radio waves to send data at rates of 11 to 300 Mbps, or up to, in theory, 1 Gbps with the latest devices (although all of these are theoretical top speeds).

There are also hardware items required:

- **Network adapter** – Appropriate to the network type, with one for each computer in the network.

- **Network controller** – One or more hub, switch or router, providing the actual connection to each network adapter.

There is also an internet connection using:

- A router that connects to the internet wirelessly (using Wi-Fi) or with a cable (Ethernet).

- A modem connected to the computer and the network (this is an increasingly outdated method).

Setting up the components

The steps you will need will depend on the specific options on your system. However, the main steps will include:

- Set up or verify the internet connection. This should be provided by your Internet Service Provider (ISP).

- Configure the wireless router or access point. Most Wi-Fi routers will be automatically recognized by Windows 11.

- Start up Windows on your laptop.

Windows 11 is designed to automate as much of the network setup task as possible.

Going Wireless

For networking, "wireless" means connecting your laptop to other devices using radio waves rather than cables. These can include a router for connecting to a network, a printer, keyboard, mouse or speakers (as long as these devices also have a wireless capability). For the laptop user in particular, this gives you the ultimate freedom: you can take your laptop wherever you want, and still be able to access the internet and use a variety of peripherals.

Wireless standards

As with everything in the world of computers, there are industry standards for wireless connections: for networking devices, the standard is known as IEEE 802.11. The purpose of standards is to ensure that all connected devices can communicate with each other.

The IEEE 802.11 standard (or just 802.11) used for networks has a number of different variations (known as protocols) of the original standard. These variations have been developed since the introduction of 802.11 in 1997, with a view to making it work faster and cover a greater range. Early wireless devices used the 802.11a and 802.11b protocols, while the most widely used protocol at the time of printing is 802.11n, with 802.11ac also beginning to be used. When you are creating a wireless network it is best to have all of the devices using the same version of 802.11. For instance, if you have a wireless card in your laptop that uses 802.11n, then it is best to have the same version in your router. However, most modern wireless cards and routers have multiple compatibility and can cater for at least the b and g versions of the standard. If two devices use different 802.11 protocols, they should still be able to communicate, but the rate of data transfer may be slower than if both of the devices used the same protocol.

The Bluetooth standard is another method of connecting devices wirelessly. It does not have the same range as 802.11 and is now mainly used for connecting devices over short distances, such as a wireless mouse.

Very few new devices use the 802.11a version of the standard, although newer devices will usually be backward-compatible with it.

Devices using the 802.11n protocol can communicate with each other via radio waves over distances of approximately 25 yards (indoors) and 75 yards (outdoors).

Connecting to a Network

You can connect your computers to form a network using Ethernet cables and adapters, or by setting up wireless adapters and routers. When you start up each computer, Windows 11 will examine the current configuration and discover any new networks that have been established since the last startup. You can check this, or connect manually to a network, from within the Wi-Fi settings from the Network & internet section of Settings. To do this:

Beware

The most common type of network for connecting to is the internet.

Beware

If your network is unavailable for any reason, this will be noted in Step 2.

152

1 Open the **Settings** app and click on the **Network & internet** tab

2 With no network currently connected, drag the **Wi-Fi** button **On**

Network & internet

Not connected
You aren't connected to any networks   Troubleshoot

Wi-Fi
Connect, manage known networks, metered network   On

Ethernet
Authentication, IP and DNS settings, metered network

3 Click on the **Show available networks** option

Show available networks

Network & internet › Wi-Fi

Wi-Fi   On

Show available networks   ⌄

4 Click on the required network

PLUSNET-TXJ5
PLUSNET-TXJ5-5g
Secured
☑ Connect automatically
                                                        Connect
Virgin Media

5 Click on the **Connect** button

6 Enter the password for the router to be used to connect to the Wi-Fi network

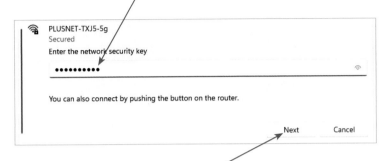

7 Click on the **Next** button

8 If the connection is successful, the network name is shown as **Connected**

9 Connected networks are shown at the top of the **Network & internet** settings window

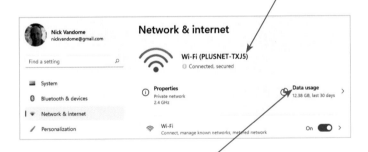

10 Click on the **Data usage** button to see which apps are using the most data on the network

If you are using a public hotspot Wi-Fi connection, such as in a cafe or an airport, this may not be as secure as your home network.

Viewing Network Status

Once you have connected to a network, and usually the internet too, you can view your current network status and apply certain settings. To do this:

1 From the main **Network & internet** settings page, click on the **Properties** button for the currently connected network

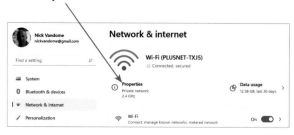

Don't forget

Click on the **Advanced network settings** option on the main **Network & internet** page to view details about the elements that make up networks in Windows.

2 Check **On** either the **Public network** or the **Private network** option to hide your device on the network (**Public** network) or make it discoverable for sharing items with other people (**Private** network)

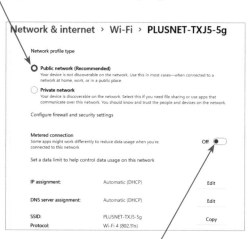

3 Drag the **Metered connection** button **Off** to reduce the amount of data that is processed across the network, if you have a limited data Wi-Fi service (Windows applies the required settings for reducing the data usage)

Sharing Settings

Options for specifying how items are shared over a network can be selected in the Network and Sharing Center. To access these (from the Settings app):

1 Open the **Settings** app, enter "**sharing settings**" into the Search box and click on the **Manage advanced sharing settings** option

2 Select sharing options for different networks, including **Private**, **Guest or Public**, and **All Networks**. Options can be selected for turning on network discovery so that your laptop can see other computers on the network, and for file and printer sharing

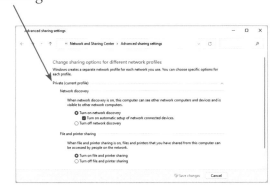

If you are sharing over a network you should be able to access the **Public** folder on another computer (providing that network discovery is turned **On**). If you are the administrator of the other computer you will also be able to access your own **Home** folder, although you will need to enter the required password for this.

3 Click on these arrowheads to expand the options for each network category

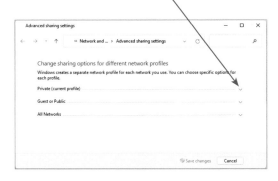

Nearby Sharing

Nearby sharing can be used to share files wirelessly, either using Bluetooth or Wi-Fi. As the name suggests, the computer with which you want to share files has to be relatively close to the one that is sharing the content. Also, the other device has to support Nearby sharing; i.e. be running a compatible version of Windows 11.
To use Nearby sharing:

If your laptop does not have Wi-Fi or Bluetooth capability, the **Nearby sharing** option will not be available.

1 Open the **Settings** app and click on the **System** tab

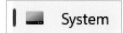

2 Click on the **Nearby sharing** option

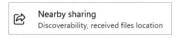

3 Click here in the **Nearby sharing** option

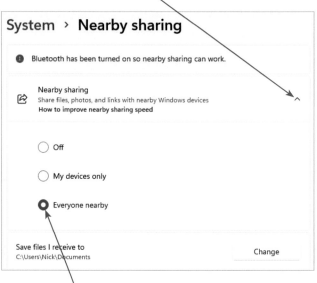

4 Select who you want to be able to share content with on your laptop. It can be everyone, or only your own devices; i.e. ones on which you have signed in with your Microsoft Account details

5 Under the **Save files I receive to** heading, in Step 3 on the previous page, click on the **Change** button to select a new location

Save files I receive to	
C:\Users\Nick\Documents	Change

6 Select a new location for files that are shared with Nearby sharing and click on the **Select Folder** button

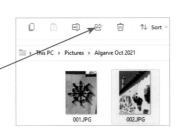

Select Folder

Sharing files

Once Nearby sharing has been set up, it can be used to share files wirelessly with other compatible devices. To do this:

1 Open File Explorer and select a file. Click on the **Share** button on the Menu bar

2 Select an option for sharing the item with someone else, including **Nearby sharing**, as shown on the previous page. Items can also be shared via email, social media and online storage apps

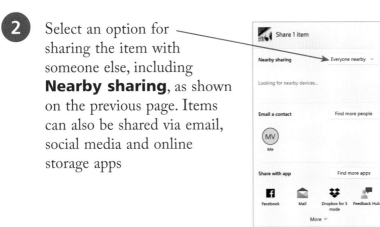

Don't forget

Both devices have to be set up for **Nearby sharing** for it to work effectively.

Network Troubleshooting

1 Open the **Settings** app, enter "**network troubleshoot**" into the Search box and click on the **Find and fix network problems** option

For more general troubleshooting options, see pages 172-173.

2 Click on the option that most closely matches your network problem

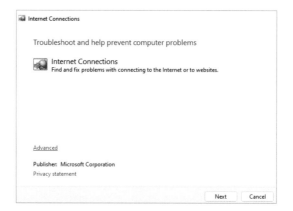

3 Most options have additional selections that can be made to try to solve the problem. Click on these as required

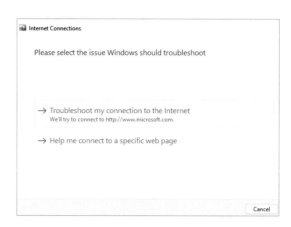

10 Battery Issues

Battery power is crucial to a laptop, and this chapter shows how to get the best out of your battery, keep it in good condition and deal with potential problems.

160 Types of Battery

161 Power Consumption

162 Battery Management

164 Battery Saver

165 Charging the Battery

166 Removing the Battery

167 Dead and Spare Batteries

168 Battery Troubleshooting

Types of Battery

A laptop's battery is one of the items that helps to define its identity: without it, the portable nature of the laptop would be very different as it would always have to be connected with a power cable. Laptops have used a variety of different types of batteries since they were first produced, and over the years these have become smaller, lighter and more powerful. However, laptop batteries are still relatively heavy and bulky, and are one of the major sources of weight in the machine:

Don't forget

The type of battery provided with a laptop, and the approximate lifespan for each charge, should be displayed with the details about the machine on the manufacturer's website or in any promotional literature that comes with it.

The main types of batteries used in modern laptops are:

- **Lithium-ion**. This is a type of battery that has a good weight-to-power ratio and loses its charge at a relatively slow rate. However, it can be prone to overheating if it is not treated properly or is defective.

- **Lithium polymer**. This is an advanced version of the lithium-ion battery. It is generally considered to be a more stable design.

Don't forget

The quality of laptop batteries is improving all the time.

These types of batteries are rechargeable, so they can be charged and used numerous times after they initially run out. However, over time, all rechargeable batteries eventually wear out and have to be replaced.

Power Consumption

Battery life for each charge of laptop batteries is one area on which engineers have worked very hard since laptops were first introduced. For most modern laptops, the average battery life for each charge is approximately between three and five hours. However, this is dependent on the power consumption of the laptop; i.e. how much power is being used to perform particular tasks. Power-intensive tasks will reduce the battery life of each charge cycle. These types of tasks include:

- Surfing the web.

- Streaming movies and TV shows.

- Editing digital photographs.

- Editing digital video.

When you are using your laptop, you can always monitor how much battery power you currently have available. This is shown by moving the cursor over the battery icon that is at the right-hand side of the Taskbar:

Beware

If you are undertaking an energy-intensive task such as browsing the web, try to use the external AC/DC power adapter rather than the battery, otherwise the battery may drain quickly and the laptop will close down.

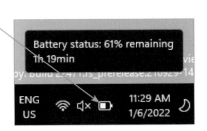

Because of the vital role that the battery plays in relation to your laptop, it is important to try to conserve its power as much as possible. To do this:

- Where possible, use the mains adapter rather than the battery when using your laptop.

- Use the **Sleep** function when you are not actively using your laptop.

- Use power-management functions to save battery power (see pages 162-163).

Battery Management

Unlike desktop computers, laptops have options for how the battery is managed. These allow you to set things like individual power schemes for the battery and to view how much charge is left in the battery. This can be done from the Settings app. To access the options for managing your laptop's battery:

1 Access the **Settings** app and click on the **System** tab

2 Click on the **Power & battery** option

3 Under the **Power** section, click on the **Screen and sleep** option to make selections for the period of inactivity

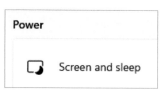

until the screen goes to sleep, for both on battery power and when connected to the mains power. Click here to select a time period for a specific state; e.g. **On battery power, turn off my screen after**

4 Select a time period for the selection made in Step 3

Don't forget

It is more important to set a shorter time for putting the screen and the laptop to sleep on battery power, as opposed to when it is on mains power.

...cont'd

5 Make selections in the same way as in Step 3 on the previous page for other options; e.g. on mains power and for putting the device to sleep

6 Click here and select a time period for the selection made in Step 5, in the same way as for putting the screen to sleep (this can include **Never**, in which case the selected option will not be put to sleep)

Power settings
Additional power settings can be made from the Power mode option. To do this:

1 Click on the **Power mode** option in the **Power & battery** section

2 Click here to select a power mode

3 Power mode offers options for **Best power efficiency**, **Balanced**, which provides the best overall combination, or **Best performance**

Beware

If you don't protect your laptop with a Microsoft Account password for when it is woken from sleep, anyone could access your folders and files if they wake the laptop from sleep. This can be specified in **Settings** > **Accounts** > **Sign-in options** – under the **If you've been away, when should Windows require you to sign in again** heading, select the **When PC wakes up from sleep** option from the drop-down menu.

163

Battery Saver

Within System settings there are also options for viewing the current level of battery charge; the estimated time remaining on the current charge; and viewing battery usage by app. There is also an option for turning the battery saver on automatically. To do this:

When the battery saver is **On**, the battery icon on the Taskbar is displayed as this icon:

1 Click on the **Power & battery** button within **Settings** > **System**

2 The current battery usage is shown here, with the estimated time remaining for the current battery charge below

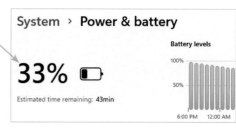

3 Click on the **Battery saver** heading to view options for saving battery power

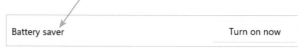

4 Select battery saver options as required. Click on the **Turn off now** button (or the **Turn on now button**) to turn the battery saver **Off** and **On**

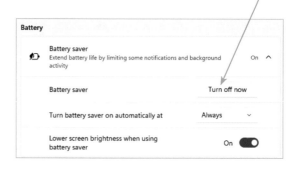

When the battery saver is **On**, background activity (such as pushing notifications and emails) is limited in order to save power.

Charging the Battery

Laptop batteries are charged using an AC/DC adapter, which can also be used to power the laptop instead of the battery. If the laptop is turned on and being powered by the AC/DC adapter, the battery will be charged at the same time, although at a slower rate than if it is being charged with the laptop turned off.

The AC/DC adapter should be supplied with a new laptop, and consists of a cable and a power adapter. To charge a laptop battery using an AC/DC adapter:

1 Connect the AC/DC adapter to the cable and plug it into the mains socket

2 Attach the AC/DC adapter to the laptop and turn it on at the mains socket

3 When the laptop is connected to the power adapter and being charged, the **Battery Meter** icon is visible at the right-hand side of the Taskbar

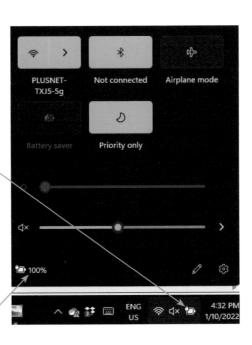

4 Click here to access the full range of battery settings

A laptop battery can be charged whether the laptop is turned on or off.

If the laptop is on battery power, click on the **Battery saver** button in Step 3 to turn this option **On**.

Removing the Battery

Although a laptop's battery does not have to be removed on a regular basis, there may be occasions when you want to do this. These include:

- If the laptop freezes; i.e. you are unable to undertake any operations using the keyboard or mouse, and you cannot turn off the laptop using the Power button.

- If you are traveling, particularly in extreme temperatures. In situations such as this, you may prefer to keep the battery with you to try to avoid exposing it to either very hot or very cold temperatures.

Laptop batteries can be removed from the back of the laptop: older models of laptop sometimes have a sliding lock that is used to access the battery compartment, while the compartment for newer laptops is usually secured with screws. To remove a laptop battery:

Some laptops, particularly slim ultrabooks, do not have removable batteries, and they have to be replaced by the manufacturer. If in doubt about how to remove the battery, consult the manufacturer's guidelines, which are usually available from their website.

1 With the laptop turned off and the lid closed, turn the laptop upside down

2 Locate the battery compartment and either push or slide the lock that keeps the battery cover in place or unscrew the screws holding the cover in place

To re-insert the battery or to insert a new battery, push it gently into the battery compartment until it clicks firmly into place.

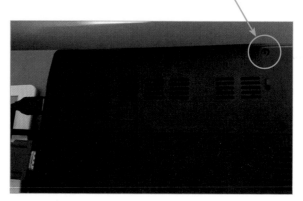

3 Slide the battery out of its compartment

Dead and Spare Batteries

No energy source lasts forever, and laptop batteries are no exception to this rule. Over time, the battery will operate less efficiently until it will not be possible to charge the battery at all. With average usage, most laptop batteries should last approximately five years, although they will start to lose performance before this. Some signs of a dead laptop battery are:

- Nothing happens when the laptop is turned on using just battery power.

- The laptop shuts down immediately if it is being run on the AC/DC adapter and the cord is suddenly removed.

- The battery icon shows no movement when the AC/DC adapter is connected; i.e. the battery status remains at 0% and shows as not charging at all. When the battery is running low (below 10%) a warning message will appear, prompting you to plug in the laptop.

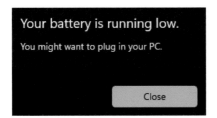

If you think that your battery may be losing its performance, make sure that you save your work at regular intervals. Although you should do this anyway, it is more important if there is a chance of your battery running out of power and abruptly turning off.

Spare battery

Because of the limited lifespan of laptop batteries, it is worth considering buying a spare battery. Although these are not cheap they can be a valuable investment, particularly if you spend a lot of time traveling with your laptop and you are not always near a source of mains electricity. In situations such as this, a spare battery could enable you to keep using your laptop if your original battery runs out of power.

When buying a spare battery, check with the laptop's manufacturer that it will be compatible: in most cases, the manufacturer will also be able to supply you with a spare battery for your laptop.

When the battery power is running low, a warning sign appears on the battery icon on the Taskbar.

If there is no response from your laptop when you turn it on in battery mode, try removing the battery and re-inserting it. If there is still no response then the battery is probably flat and should be replaced.

If you are not going to be using your laptop for an extended period of time, remove the battery and store it in a safe, dry, cool place.

Battery Troubleshooting

If you look after your laptop battery well, it should provide you with several years of mobile computing power. However, there are some problems that may occur with the battery:

- **It won't keep its charge even when connected to an AC/DC adapter**. The battery is probably flat and should be replaced.

- **It only charges up a limited amount**. Over time, laptop batteries become less efficient and so do not hold their charge so well. One way to try to improve this is to drain the battery completely before it is charged again.

- **It keeps its charge but runs down quickly**. This can be caused by the use of a lot of power-hungry applications on the laptop. The more work the laptop has to do to run applications, such as those involving videos or games, the more power will be required from the battery and the faster it will run down.

- **It is fully charged but does not appear to work at all when inserted**. Check that the battery has clicked into place properly in the battery compartment and that the battery and laptop terminals are clean and free from dust or moisture.

- **It is inserted correctly but still does not work**. The battery may have become damaged in some way, such as becoming very wet. If you know the battery is damaged in any way, do not insert it, as it could short-circuit the laptop. If the battery has been in contact with liquid, dry it out completely before you try inserting it into the laptop. If it is dried thoroughly, it may work again.

- **It gets very hot when in operation**. This could be caused by a faulty battery, and it can be dangerous and lead to a fire. If in doubt, turn off the laptop immediately and consult the manufacturer. In some cases faulty laptop batteries are recalled, so keep an eye on the manufacturer's website to see if there are any details of this if you are concerned.

11 System and Security

Windows 11 includes tools to help protect your online privacy, troubleshoot common problems and protect your laptop from malicious software.

170 Privacy

172 Troubleshooting

174 System Properties

176 Cleaning Up Your Disk

178 Windows Update

181 Backing Up

182 System Restore

184 Windows Security

Privacy

Online privacy is a major issue for all computer users, and Windows 11 has a number of options for viewing details about your personal online privacy.

The Privacy options have been updated in Windows 11.

1 Open the **Settings** app and click on the **Privacy & security** tab

2 The **Privacy & security** options are displayed in the **Security** and **Windows permissions** sections (and the **App permissions** section further down the page; see Step 7 on the next page)

3 Click on the **General** items under the **Windows permissions** heading to select options for: allowing or denying

Click on **Privacy Statement** in Step 3 to view Microsoft's privacy statement (this is an online statement and, by default, is displayed within the Edge browser).

advertising more specific to you; letting websites provide local advertising content based on the language used within Windows; letting Windows track your app usage for improving the Start menu and search results; and showing specific results within the Settings app

4 Click on the **Search permissions** option under the **Windows permissions** heading shown in Step 2 on the previous page

> Search permissions
> SafeSearch, cloud content search, search history

5 Select options for **SafeSearch**, to specify the type of content that can be displayed from web searches

Privacy & security › **Search permissions**

To give you relevant results, Windows Search will search the web, apps, settings, and files. To change which files on your device are searched, go to Searching Windows

SafeSearch

In Windows Search, web previews will not automatically load web results if they may contain adult content. If you choose to preview web results, we'll apply the following setting:

○ Strict — Filter out adult text, images, and videos from my web results

● Moderate — Filter adult images and videos but not text from my web results

○ Off — Don't filter adult content from my web results

Hot tip

If **Find my device** in Step 6 is turned **On**, the device can be located on the web. To do this, log in to your Microsoft Account at account.microsoft.com

171

6 Under the **Security** section, select options for: **Windows Security**; **Find my device**, for locating a missing Windows 11 device; and **For developers**, for advanced users

Security

🛡 Windows Security
Antivirus, browser, firewall, and network protection for your device

⚥ Find my device
Track your device if you think you've lost it

🍴 For developers
These settings are intended for development use only

7 Under the **App permissions** section, click on specific functions and apps to set options for security and permissions

App permissions

◁ Location

📷 Camera

🎤 Microphone

Troubleshooting

On any computing system, there are always things that go wrong or do not work properly. Windows 11 is no different, but there are comprehensive troubleshooting options for trying to address a range of problems. To use these:

The troubleshooting options have been updated in Windows 11.

The **Recommended trouble-shooter preferences** in Step 2 include a range of options that are selected automatically by Windows 11.

1 Open the **Settings** app, select **System** and click on the **Troubleshoot** option

> Troubleshoot
> Recommended troubleshooters, preferences, history

2 Recommended troubleshooting options are displayed within the main window

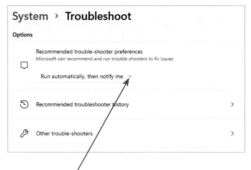

System > **Troubleshoot**

Options

Recommended trouble-shooter preferences
Microsoft can recommend and run trouble-shooters to fix issues

Run automatically, then notify me ⌄

Recommended troubleshooter history >

Other trouble-shooters >

3 Click here to select options for how the recommended troubleshooters work

Run automatically, don't notify me

Run automatically, then notify me

Ask me before running

Don't run any

4 Click on the **Recommended troubleshooter history** button in Step 2 to view the most recent troubleshooters that have been run

··· > **Recommended troubleshooter history**

🔍 Search troubleshooter
Critical troubleshooter   Ran successfully on 11/18/2020 ⌄

🔁 System Protection troubleshooter
Critical troubleshooter   Couldn't be run on 3/15/2020 ⌄

🔁 Windows Update troubleshooter
Critical troubleshooter   Ran successfully on 9/25/2019 ⌄

5 Click on the **Other trouble-shooters** button in Step 2 on the previous page to access troubleshooting options for specific hardware items and apps

System › Troubleshoot › **Other trouble-shooters**

Most frequent

	Internet Connections	Run
	Playing Audio	Run
	Printer	Run
	Windows Update	Run

Other

	Bluetooth	Run
	Camera	Run
	Connection to a Workplace Using DirectAccess	Run

Hot tip

Try the troubleshooting options first for hardware devices before you try to physically repair any problems.

173

6 Click on one of the categories to select it, and click on the **Run** button

Run

7 The troubleshooting process will run for the selected item, and a report is displayed once the troubleshooting has been completed. Click on the **Close** button

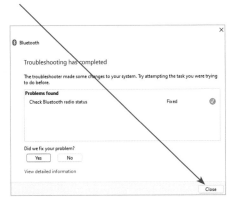

System Properties

There are several ways to open the System properties and view information about your laptop:

- Select **Settings > System > About**; or

- Press the **WinKey** + the **Pause/Break** keys; or

- Right-click **This PC** in the File Explorer Navigation pane, then select **Properties** from the menu.

The main System panel (About) provides the Windows 11 edition, processor details, memory size and device name.

Device Manager

1 Right-click on the **Start** button and click on the **Device Manager** option from the menu

Device Manager

2 Select the **>** symbol to expand that entry to show details

3 Double-click any device to open its properties (see top of the next page)

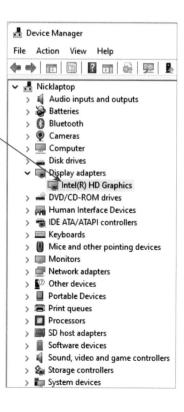

You may be prompted for an administrator password or asked for permission to continue when you select some Device Manager entries.

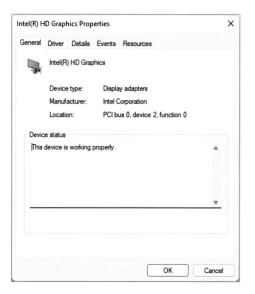

4 Select the **Driver** tab and select **Update Driver** to find and install new software

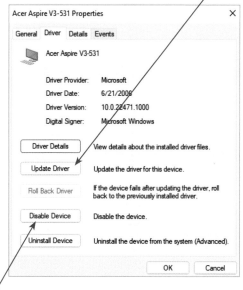

Hot tip

Click on the **Roll Back Driver** button in Step 4 (if available) to switch back to the previously installed driver for a device if the new one for it fails.

5 Select **Disable Device** to put a particular device offline. The button changes to **Enable Device**, to reverse the action

Cleaning Up Your Disk

The cleanup options within the Settings app can be used to remove items on your laptop that are no longer required, thus freeing up more space on your hard drive. To use these:

The cleanup options have been updated in Windows 11.

1 In **Settings**, select **System** > **Storage** and click on the **Cleanup recommendations** option

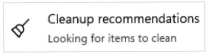

Cleanup recommendations
Looking for items to clean

2 Check **On** any items that you are happy about removing from your laptop; e.g. the contents of the **Recycle Bin**

··· › Storage › **Cleanup recommendations**

Temporary files

Recycle Bin 44.4 GB
The Recycle Bin contains files you have deleted from your computer. These files are not permanently removed until you empty the Recycle Bin.

Previous Windows installation(s) 15.7 GB
Files from a previous Windows installation. Files and folders that may conflict with the installation of Windows have been moved to folders named Windows.old. You can access data from the previous Windows installations in this folder.

Downloads 320 MB
Warning: These are files in your personal Downloads folder. Select this if you'd like to delete everything. This does not respect your Storage Sense configuration.

Cleanup will also remove system files that are not in use
See advanced options

Clean up 44.4 GB

3 Click on the **Clean up** button to remove the selected items

4 Scroll down the page to select particularly large or unused files. Select them in the same way as in Step 2 and click on the **Clean up** button to remove them

Clean up 17.5 MB

Large or unused files

Older files (2)
Name Last opened Size

C7_FullText(1).pdf 8/23/2020 11:29 AM 10.9 MB
C:\Users\Nick\Downloads

C7_FullText.pdf 8/23/2020 11:28 AM 10.9 MB
C:\Users\Nick\Downloads

Recording test-20210401_100553-Meeting Recording.mp4 4/1/2021 9:09 AM 6.66 MB
C:\Users\Nick\Downloads

Beware

If the **Recycle Bin** option is selected in Step 2, the items contained within it will be deleted permanently and will not be able to be restored.

When a file is written to the hard disk, it may be stored in several pieces in different places. This fragmentation of disk space can slow down your laptop. Disk Defragmenter rearranges the data so that the disk will work more efficiently.

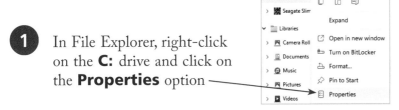

1 In File Explorer, right-click on the **C:** drive and click on the **Properties** option

Spellings are localized.

2 Select the **Tools** tab and click on the **Optimize** button

3 The process runs as a scheduled task, but you can select a drive and select **Analyze** to check out a new drive

Only disks that can be fragmented are shown. These can include USB drives that you add to your system.

4 Click the **Optimize** button to process the selected disk drive. This may take between several minutes to several hours to complete, depending on the size and state of the disk, but you can still use your laptop while the task is running

177

Windows Update

Updates to Windows 11 and other Microsoft products are supplied regularly to help prevent or fix problems, improve security or enhance performance. The way in which they are downloaded and installed can be specified in the Settings app:

Don't forget

If there are no updates displayed in Step 2, click on the **Check for updates** button. If there are updates displayed, click on the **Download now** button.

1 Open the **Settings** app and click on the **Windows Update** tab

2 There are a range of options available on the main **Windows Update** page for managing the way that updates are performed on your laptop

Hot tip

An icon for alerting you to available updates can be placed on the Taskbar, rather than having to check within the Settings app each time. To set this up, access **Settings** > **Windows Update** > **Advanced options** and drag **On** the **Notify me when a restart is required to finish updating** option. When an update is available, the icon on the Taskbar will display an orange dot.

3 Click on the **Pause for 1 week** option to stop updates being installed for seven days

4 A yellow icon appears on the **Windows Update** page, indicating that updates have been paused. Click on the **Resume updates** button to resume them again

5 Click on the **Update history** button

6 The Windows Update history is displayed, with the most recent updates at the top of the list

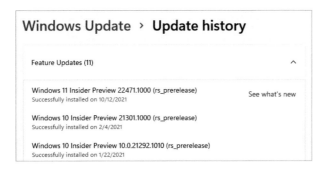

7 Click on the **Advanced options** button

8 The Advanced options include options for specifying if you receive updates about Microsoft products other than Windows 11, and for receiving notifications about restarts following an update

Drag the **Get me up to date** button **On** in Step 8 to ensure that once updates have been installed, the laptop will restart as soon as possible afterward, to complete the update. A notification will be sent 15 minutes before the restart is due.

...cont'd

9 Scroll down the **Advanced options** page to view the **Additional options** section, including **Optional updates**, which can be used for updating drivers for items such as printers, and also options for resetting Windows 11 (**Recovery**)

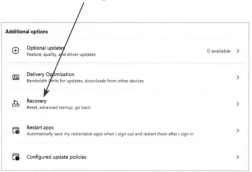

10 Click on the **Active hours** option in Step 8 on page 179

11 Select times during which your laptop won't be restarted, if an update

has been installed automatically (to prevent it from restarting when you are using it)

Hot tip

if the **Windows Insider Program** has been activated from the option in Step 12, it can be stopped by clicking on the **Stop getting preview builds** in the Windows Insider Program window.

12 Click on the **Windows Insider Program** button in Step 2 on page 178 to set up options for receiving preview copies of Windows, before a general release

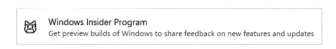

Backing Up

Backing up your data is an important task in any computer environment, and in Windows 11 this can be done from within the File History section of the Control Panel, which can also be accessed from the Settings app. To do this:

1 Connect an external storage device, such as an external hard drive, to your laptop

2 Access the **Settings** app and enter "**file history**" into the Search box and click on **Restore your files with File History**

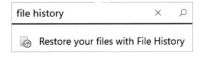

3 Click **Configure File History settings** then click the **System Image Backup** option in the bottom left-hand corner of the **File History** window that appears

4 Click on the **Set up backup** option

5 Click on the **Run now** option

6 Select the required external device for the backup and click on the **Next** button to complete the backup

Hot tip

Folders can also be backed up with the OneDrive online storage function. To do this, select **Settings** > **Accounts** > **Windows backup**. Click on the **Set up syncing** button (or the **Manage sync settings** button if syncing has already been set up) in the **OneDrive folder syncing** section, and select folders to be backed up and synced with OneDrive.

Hot tip

Files and folders can also be backed up by copying them in File Explorer and then pasting them into an external device, such as a USB flashdrive.

System Restore

Windows 11 takes snapshots of system files before any software updates are applied, or in any event once every seven days. You can also create a snapshot manually. The snapshots are known as Restore Points and are managed by System Restore.

System Restore returns system files to an earlier point in time, allowing you to undo system changes without affecting your documents, email, and other data files.

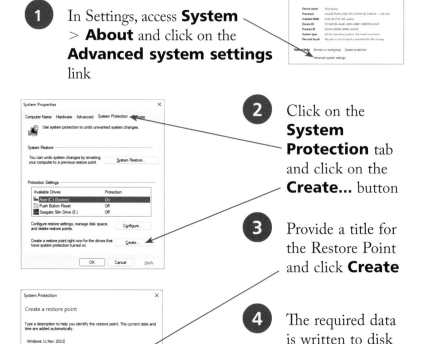

1 In Settings, access **System > About** and click on the **Advanced system settings** link

2 Click on the **System Protection** tab and click on the **Create...** button

3 Provide a title for the Restore Point and click **Create**

4 The required data is written to disk and the manual Restore Point is set up

Using Restore Points

The installation of a new app or driver software may make Windows 11 behave unpredictably. Usually, uninstalling the app or rolling back the driver (see page 175) will correct the situation. If this does not fix the problem, use an automatic or manual Restore Point to reset your system to an earlier date when everything worked correctly.

1 Select **System Protection** and click the **System Restore...** button

2 By default, this will offer to undo the most recent change. This may fix the problem

3 Otherwise, click a suitable item to use as the Restore Point

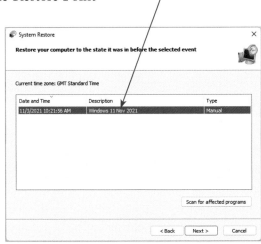

If the selected Restore Point does not resolve the problem, you can try again, selecting another Restore Point.

4 Follow the prompts to restart the system using system files from the selected date and time

Windows Security

The Windows Security app, which is pre-installed with Windows 11, can be used to give a certain amount of protection against viruses and malicious software. To use it:

1 Select **Settings** > **Privacy & security**

2 Click on the **Windows Security** option and you'll see options listed under the **Protection areas** heading

Hot tip

Click on the **Virus & threat protection** option in Step 2 to run a virus check over your laptop.

3 Click on one of the **Protection areas** categories to view its options

4 Click on the **Open Windows Security** button on the main security page to open the **Windows Security** app

Open Windows Security

5 Click each item to view its options and use the left-hand toolbar to move between sections. Click on the **Home** button to return to this page

Using a firewall

A firewall can be used to help protect your network from viruses and malicious software. To set this up:

1 Click on the **Firewall & network protection** option on the **Windows Security** Homepage

2 The related networks are listed, with their firewall status; e.g. **Firewall is on**

3 If a firewall is **Off** for any item, click on the **Turn on** button to activate it

Turn on

185

...cont'd

Protecting against viruses

The Windows Security center can be used to give a certain amount of protection against viruses and malicious software. To do this:

Malware (malicious software) is designed to deliberately harm your laptop. To protect your system, you need up-to-date antivirus and anti-spyware software. The **Windows Security** option provides this, and you can also install a separate antivirus app.

1 On the **Windows Security** Homepage, click on the **Virus & threat protection** option

2 Click on the **Quick scan** button to scan your system for viruses

Click on the **Scan options** link in Step 2 to access options for more comprehensive scans over your laptop.

Scan options

3 Once the scan is completed, any threats will be noted and options for dealing with them listed; e.g. remove or quarantine an item(s). If there are no threats, this will also be noted

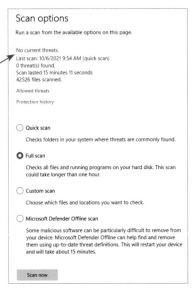

A

Accessibility
From Sign-in screen   58
Adding users.   See Users: Adding
All apps   37-38, 77
Android apps   76
Apps.   See also Windows 11 apps
About   76-77
Android   76
Buying   87
Closing   81-82
Installing   89
Maximizing   81
Menus   81
Microsoft Store   84-88
Microsoft Store apps   76
Minimizing   81
Moving   80
Pin to Start menu   39
Reinstalling   88
Searching for   83
Uninstalling   90
Using   80-81
Windows 11 apps   76
Windows classic apps   76

B

Background
Changing the Desktop background 44
Setting   44-45
Backing up   181
With OneDrive   181
Backpack   130
Battery
AC/DC adapter   165
Battery saver   164
Charging   165
Icon   161

Life   161
Lithium-ion   160
Lithium polymer   160
Management   162-163
Power   10
Rechargeable   160
Re-inserting   166
Removing   166
Spare   25, 167
Troubleshooting   168
Bookmarking web pages   98
Buying apps   87

C

Calendar   116-118
Adding events   117-118
Carry case   24
CD/DVD
Players and re-writers   21
CD writers   13
Central processing unit (CPU)   12
Chat app   33, 136-138
Adding emojis   138
Attach Files   138
Formatting text   138
Get started   136
Cleaning material   26
Cleaning up your disk   176-177
Closing an app   82
Color themes
Changing   52-53
Connectivity.   See Laptops: Connectivity
Cookies   102
On online shopping sites   102-103
Cortana   64-67
Searching with   65-66
Settings   67
Setting up   64
Using   65-67

D

Dark color theme	53
Desktop	40
Accessing	35
Accessing with shortcuts	40
Desktop background	44-45
Fitting size for photos	45
Device Manager	174-175
Disk defragmenter	177
Dry-bags	133
DVDs/CDs	26
DVD writers	13

E

Edge browser. *See* Microsoft Edge browser	
Emojis	109
In Chat app	138
Energy-intensive tasks	161
Ethernet	21, 150

F

Family history	105
Family Safety	144-148
Apps and games controls	147
Recent activity controls	145
Screen time controls	148
Web-browsing controls	145-146
File Explorer	70-74
Menu bar	73-74
New	74
Share	74
View	74
Opening	70
Quick access	71-72
Firewall	185
Flashdrives	56
Focus assist	68

G

Gaming	128
Achievements	128
Activity feed	128
Clubs	128
My games	128
Genealogy	105
Gmail	106
Graphical user interface (GUI)	30
Graphics card. *See* Laptops: Graphics card	
Groove Music app	124

H

Hand position	19
HDMI (High-Definition Multimedia Interface)	21
Headphones	26
Hotspots	22
Hybrids	11

I

IBM	8-9
IEEE 802.11	151
Installing apps	89
Internet Explorer (IE)	92

K

Keyboard	19

L

Language
  Display 64
  Speech 64
Laptop case 130
Laptop position 16
Laptops
  Avoiding water 133
  Carrying 18
  Cleaning 23
  Connectivity 13
  Desktop replacements 11
  Drying out 133
  Functionality 10
  Graphics card 13
  Hybrids 11
  IBM-compatible 9
  Insulating against heat 132
  Keeping dry 133
  Memory 12
  Netbooks 11
  Notebooks 11
  Optical drive 13
  Pointing device 13
  Portability 10
  Ports 13
  Power 10
  Processor 12
  Safety on vacation 131
  Screen sizes 11
  Size 14
  Storage 12
  Transporting 130
  Ultrabooks 11
  Webcam 13
  Weight 14
  Wireless 13
Light color theme 52
Local Account
  Signing in with 59
Locking your laptop 58
Lock screen 58
  Settings 48-49
Logging in 58-59
Luggables 9

M

Mail 106-109
  Accounts 106-107
  Formatting 109
  POP3 account 106
  Sending 108-109
  Setting up 106-107
Malware 186
Memory. *See* Laptops: Memory
Memory card reader 21
Metal case 130
Microsoft Account 42-43
  Creating 42-43
  Email address 142-143
  Prompted to create 42
  Services 42
Microsoft Edge browser 99-101
  About 92
  Bookmarking pages 98
  Collections 100-101
  Homepage 94
  Settings 94
  Smart address bar 93
  Tabs 95
    Managing 96-97
    Vertical tabs 96-97
Microsoft Store
  About 84-86
  Buying apps 87
  Library 88
  Ratings and reviews 85
  Reinstalling apps 88
  Viewing your apps 88
Microsoft Store apps 77
Microsoft Surface Pro 29
Microsoft Teams 33
Microsoft website for Windows 11 31
Mouse
  External 20, 26
  Wireless 20
Movies and TV
  Viewing 126-127
MS-DOS 30
Multi-card reader 21, 26

Multiple users
    Customization   141
    Overview   140-141
Music
    Playing   125

N

Nearby sharing   156-157
Network
    Available networks   152
    Components   150
    Connecting to   152-153
    Troubleshooting   158
Networking
    Wireless   151
Notifications   68-69
    Settings   69

O

OneDrive
    Adding items in File Explorer   111
    Adding items to OneDrive online   112
    Adding items in the OneDrive app   112
    Online   110-111
    Overview   110-111
    Personal Vault   110
    Settings   113
Opening a laptop   28
Optical drive.   See Laptops: Optical drive
Outlook   106

P

Padlock   24
Parental controls.   See Family Safety
Pausing updates   178

People app   114-115
    Adding contacts manually   115
    Finding   114-115
    Pinning contacts   115
Personalization   44-47
    Background   44-45
    Colors   46-47
Photos
    App   120-123
    Draw button   122
    Editing   122-123
    Importing   120
    Viewing   120-121
Pinning apps   39
Pinning to Start menu   39
Pin to taskbar   39
Pointing device. See Laptops: Pointing device
Ports.   See Laptops: Ports
Posture   15
Power
    Conserving   161
    Usage   161
Power cable   25
Power off button   58
Power options   34
Power sockets   134
Pre-installed Windows   31
Privacy   170-171
    App permissions   171
    Find my device   171
    For developers   171
    Privacy statement   170
    Search permissions   171
    Windows permissions   170-171
    Windows Security   171
Processor.   See Laptops: Processor

Q

Quick access
    Pinning items   72
Quick Settings   60

R

Random-access memory (RAM)   12
Removing users.   *See* Users: Removing
Restart   36, 41
    For updates   41
Restore points   182-183
Ribbon.   *See* Scenic Ribbon

S

Scanning for viruses   186
Scenic Ribbon
    Replaced in File Explorer   73
Screen adjusting   17
Screen glare   17
Screen resolution   54
Searching   62-63
    Asking a question   63
    Over your laptop   63
    Text search   62
Seating position   15
Security at airports   135
Settings   60-61
    Accessing   60
    Adding to the Taskbar   60
    Quick Settings   60
Sharing files   157
Shopping online   102-103
Shoulder strap   24
Shutting down   36, 41
    From the Start button   41
    From the Start menu   41
Sign-in options   58-59
    Facial recognition   59
    Fingerprint recognition   59
Sign-in settings   59
Sign out   36, 41
Skype   137
Sleep   36, 41
Snapshots with System Restore   182
Spotify   125

Start button   34-35
    Functionality   35
    In previous versions   77
    Shutting down from the Start menu and
        Start button   41
    Updated   32
    Using   34
Start menu   36-39, 41
    All apps   37-38
    Back button   37
    Color   32
    Most used   37
    Pinned apps   36, 39
    Power button   36
    Recommended items   36
    Restart   36, 41
    Shut down or sign out   36, 41
    Shutting down   36, 41
    Sleep   36, 41
    Updated   32
Storage.   *See* Laptops: Storage
Structure of the Desktop   40
System properties   174-175
    Device Manager   174-175
System Restore   182-183
    For creating Restore Points   182-183

T

Tablets   29
Tabs
    Using in Microsoft Edge   95
Taskbar   40
    Notifications area   40
    Viewing open windows   40
Temperature extremes   132
Themes   50-51
This PC
    For accessing Properties   174
Touchpad   19
Touchscreens   29
Travel   104-105
Troubleshooting   158, 172-173
Turning off   41

U

Uninstalling apps	90
Unpinning apps	39
Updates	
Restarting	41
Universal Serial Bus (USB)	13, 21
USB flashdrive	26
USB Type-C	21
Users	
Adding	142-143
Removing	143
Using Restore Points	182-183

V

Vacation	
Booking	104-105
Cruises	105
Hotels	105
Viruses	186
Voice searching with Cortana	65-66
Volume adjustments	55

W

Webcam.	See Laptops: Webcam
Web searches	63
Widgets	33
Wi-Fi	22
Connecting to a network	152-153
Windows 11	9
About	30
Installing	31
Obtaining	31
Windows 11 apps	77-79
Alarms & Clock	78
Calculator	78
Calendar	78
Camera	78
Groove Music	78
Mail	78
Maps	78
Microsoft Edge	78
Microsoft News	78
Microsoft Store	78-79
Microsoft Teams	78
Microsoft To Do	78
Movies & TV	79
OneDrive	79
OneNote	79
Outlook	79
Paint 3D	79
Photos	79
Settings	79
Snipping Tool	79
Sticky Notes	79
Voice Recorder	79
Weather	79
Xbox	79
Windows 11 Installation Assistant	31
Windows Security	184-186
Firewall & network protection	185
Protection areas	184
Quick scan	186
Virus & threat protection	184, 186
Windows Update	178-180
Active hours	180
Advanced options	179
For obtaining Windows 11	31
Get me up to date	179
Pausing updates	178
Resuming updates	178
Update history	179
Windows Insider Program	180
Windows updates restarting	41
WinKey (Windows key)	40, 70, 109
Wireless 22.	See also Laptops: Wireless
Wireless networking	151-153
Working position	15-17
Wrong password when signing in	58

X

Xbox	79, 128